Nonfiction Writers Dig Deep

NCTE Editorial Board

Nonfiction Writers Dig Deep

50 Award-Winning Children's Book Authors Share the Secret of Engaging Writing

Edited by
Melissa Stewart

NATIONAL COUNCIL OF TEACHERS OF ENGLISH
340 N. NEIL ST., SUITE #104, CHAMPAIGN, ILLINOIS 61820
WWW.NCTE.ORG

Portions of this book were adapted from Stewart, M., & Young, T. A. (2019). Teaching the key traits of expository nonfiction with children's books. *The Reading Teacher, 72*(5), 648–51. Used by permission of John Wiley and Sons.

A portion of the royalties generated from the sale of this publication will be assigned by the editor to We Need Diverse Books (WNDB) and the Society of Children's Book Writers and Illustrators (SCBWI).

Staff Editor: Bonny Graham
Interior Design: Jenny Jensen Greenleaf
Cover Design: Pat Mayer

NCTE Stock Number: 33521; eStock Number: 33545
ISBN 978-0-8141-3352-1; eISBN 978-0-8141-3354-5

It is the policy of NCTE in its journals and other publications to provide a forum for the open discussion of ideas concerning the content and the teaching of English and the language arts. Publicity accorded to any particular point of view does not imply endorsement by the Executive Committee, the Board of Directors, or the membership at large, except in announcements of policy, where such endorsement is clearly specified.

NCTE provides equal employment opportunity to all staff members and applicants for employment without regard to race, color, religion, sex, national origin, age, physical, mental or perceived handi-cap/disability, sexual orientation including gender identity or expression, ancestry, genetic information, marital status, military status, unfavorable discharge from military service, pregnancy, citizenship status, personal appearance, matriculation or political affiliation, or any other protected status under applicable federal, state, and local laws.

Every effort has been made to provide current URLs and email addresses, but, because of the rapidly changing nature of the web, some sites and addresses may no longer be accessible.

Library of Congress Cataloging-in-Publication Data

Names: Stewart, Melissa, editor.
Title: Nonfiction writers dig deep : award-winning children's book authors share the secret of engaging writing / edited by Melissa Stewart.
Description: Champaign, Illinois : National Council of Teachers of English, 2020. | Includes biblio-graphical references and index. | Summary: "Celebrated authors share essays that describe a critical part of the informational writing process that is often left out of classroom instruction, helping stu-dents to craft rich, unique prose"—Provided by publisher.
Identifiers: LCCN 2020027095 (print) | LCCN 2020027096 (ebook) | ISBN 9780814133521 (trade paper-back) | ISBN 9780814133545 (adobe pdf)
Subjects: LCSH: Children's literature—Authorship. | Creative nonfiction—Authorship. | Creative nonfiction—Technique. | English language—Composition and exercises—Study and teaching (Elementary) | English language—Composition and exercises—Study and teaching (Middle school)
Classification: LCC PN147.5 .N66 2020 (print) | LCC PN147.5 (ebook) | DDC 808.06/8—dc23
LC record available at https://lccn.loc.gov/2020027095
LC ebook record available at https://lccn.loc.gov/2020027096

To educators who spark a love of literacy through their never-ending quest to find the right book, for the right child, at the right time.

—M. S.

Contents

Guide to Children's Literature Book Awards

AAAS/Subaru Book Prize = American Association for the Advancement of Science/Subaru *SB&F* Prize for Excellence in Science Books, administered by AAAS and Subaru of America

ALA Notable = American Library Association Notable Books for Children, administered by the Association for Library Service to Children, a division of the American Library Association

APALA Literature Award = Asian/Pacific American Award for Literature, administered by the Asian/Pacific American Librarians Association

Boston Globe–Horn Book Award, administered by *The Horn Book*

Caldecott Award = Randolph Caldecott Medal, administered by the Association for Library Service to Children, a division of the American Library Association

Carter G. Woodson Book Award, administered by the National Council for the Social Studies

CCBC Choices = Cooperative Children's Book Center Choices, administered by the Cooperative Children's Book Center, University of Wisconsin-Madison School of Education

The Christopher Award, administered by the Christophers

The Cook Prize, administered by the Bank Street College of Education and *School Library Journal*

Coretta Scott King Book Award, administered by the American Library Association

Crystal Kite Award, administered by the Society of Children's Book Writers and Illustrators

E. B. White Read Aloud Award, administered by the Association of Booksellers for Children

Flora Stieglitz Straus Award, administered by the Bank Street College of Education

Golden Kite Award, administered by the Society of Children's Book Writers and Illustrators

Green Earth Book Award, administered by The Nature Generation

Gryphon Award, administered by the Center for Children's Books at the School of Information Sciences at the University of Illinois at Urbana-Champaign

Jane Addams Children's Book Award, administered by the Jane Addams Peace Association

Los Angeles Times Book Prize, administered by the *Los Angeles Times*

Mathical Book Prize, administered by the Mathematical Sciences Research Institute in partnership with the National Council of Teachers of English and the National Council of Teachers of Mathematics and in coordination with the Children's Book Council

NAACP Image Award = National Association for the Advancement of Colored People Image Award, administered by the NAACP Hollywood Bureau

National Book Award, administered by the National Book Foundation

Newbery Award = John Newbery Medal, administered by the Association for Library Service to Children, a division of the American Library Association

NSTA Best STEM Book = National Science Teaching Association Best STEM Books K–12, administered by NSTA and the Children's Book Council

NSTA Outstanding Science Trade Book = National Science Teaching Association Outstanding Science Trade Books for Students in K–12, administered by NSTA and the Children's Book Council

Orbis Pictus Award, administered by the National Council of Teachers of English

PEN/Steven Kroll Award for Picture Book Writing, administered by PEN America

Printz Award = Michael L. Printz Award for Excellence in Young Adult Literature, administered by the Young Adult Library Services Association, a division of the American Library Association

Schneider Family Book Award, administered by the American Library Association

Scott O'Dell Award for Historical Fiction, administered by Elizabeth Hall, widow of children's book author Scott O'Dell

Sibert Award = Robert F. Sibert Informational Book Medal, administered by the Association for Library Service to Children, a division of the American Library Association

Social Justice Literature Award, administered by the International Literacy Association's Literacy and Social Responsibility Special Interest Group

Sugarman Award = Norman A. Sugarman Children's Biography Award, administered by the Cleveland Public Library

Sydney Taylor Book Award, administered by the Association of Jewish Libraries

YALSA Nonfiction Award = Young Adult Library Services Association Award for Excellence in Nonfiction for Young Adults, administered by YALSA, a division of the American Library Association

Acknowledgments

Thank you to Alyson Beecher for moderating the NCTE panel that provided the initial spark for this anthology and to all the children's books authors who contributed essays. Many people warned me that overseeing a project that includes fifty writers with busy schedules was an act of insanity, but you made it easy.

I'd also like to thank Terrell Young for suggesting NCTE as a publisher and Franki Sibberson for helping me make contact with Robb Clouse, who acquired the book and patiently guided it through the early stages of the editorial process. I'm also grateful to staff editor Bonny Graham, publications director Kurt Austin, designer Jenny Jensen Greenleaf, cover designer Pat Mayer, and the entire NCTE Books Program staff for their contributions. Thanks also go to Patricia Newman for taking the time to read an early version of the manuscript and offer valuable suggestions, to Gerard Fairley for his administrative assistance, and to Mary Ann Cappiello for offering sage advice at just the right moment.

And finally I'd like to extend my gratitude to Kelsey Bond, Pete Frew, Heather Gallagher Photography, and Hugh Smith for granting permission to use photographs they took of the contributing authors, and to all the publishers (Albert Whitman; Bloomsbury; Boyds Mills Press & Kane; Candlewick; Charlesbridge; Chronicle; Creston; Eerdrmans; Hachette; HarperCollins; Holiday House; Houghton Mifflin Harcourt; Lee & Low; Lerner; Macmillan; National Geographic; Peachtree; Penguin Random House; Roost; Scholastic; Simon & Schuster; Sourcebooks; and Sterling) that allowed the contributing authors to include book cover images in their essays.

Introduction

Why We Wrote This Book

You might be wondering why a group of fifty nonfiction children's book authors have come together to create a book for educators. After all, most of the time, we choose to write for kids.

Our motive is simple. We've noticed a critical gap in nonfiction writing instruction, and we'd like to help you make the student writing process more authentic.

As author Laura Purdie Salas states in her essay on page 71, "[T]here's a common, crushing misconception that fiction is creative writing drawn from the depths of a writer's soul, while nonfiction is simply a recitation of facts that any basic robot could spit out."

We aren't sure why many teachers and students seem to think that writing nonfiction requires nothing more than doing some research and cobbling together a bunch of facts, but we'd like to pull back the curtain on our prewriting process to reveal the truth. The topics we choose, the approaches we take, and the concepts and themes we explore are closely linked to who we are as people—our passions, our personalities, our beliefs, and our experiences in the world. As far as we're concerned, putting the information we collect through our own personal filters and making our own meaning is the secret to creating engaging nonfiction.

Consider these brief excerpts from essays included later in this book:

> Writing nonfiction is a highly personal experience for me—a journey. And the adventure begins with a strong connection to my topic. While the connection could be rooted in passion, it might also stem from intense curiosity . . . or fear.
> —Heather Lang, author of the 2017 NSTA Best STEM Book,
> *Fearless Flyer: Ruth Law and Her Flying Machine*

I study my subject's lives, trying to understand their inner truth. I need to know what makes them tick. But I also consider what makes me tick—my inner truth. When our truths are in alignment, that's a story I feel that I can tell.

—Don Tate, author-illustrator of the 2016 Carter G. Woodson Book Award winner *Poet: The Remarkable Story of George Moses Horton*

Just as fiction authors write about themes that resonate with them, so too do nonfiction authors. My themes first have to light *my* fire with a personal connection.

—Patricia Newman, author of the 2018 Sibert Honor title *Sea Otter Heroes: The Predators That Saved an Ecosystem*

I want my books to describe scientific concepts *and* elicit an emotional response from readers. To achieve this, I draw on the connections I forged with the subject during the research process.

—Jason Chin, author-illustrator of the 2018 Sibert Honor and Caldecott Honor title *Grand Canyon*

[T]he true tales I write spring directly from my experiences, passions, heartbreaks, obsessions, fears, quirks, curiosities, beliefs, desires. Writing nonfiction is like sitting before a blank screen and scraping off a piece of myself.

—Candace Fleming, author of the 2014 Orbis Pictus Award winner, *The Family Romanov: Murder, Rebellion, and the Fall of Imperial Russia.*

Simply put, to create high-quality nonfiction, writers need to have skin in the game. They need to dig deep and find a personal connection to their topic and their approach. If your students' nonfiction writing seems dull and lifeless, it's probably because they don't feel invested in the process or the product. Our goal in writing this book is to change that.

The Evolution of an Idea

To be honest, for a long time even we didn't fully understand or appreciate this important aspect of our creative process. Since nobody ever talked about it, we didn't recognize that it's something we all have in common.

That began to change at the 2017 National Council of Teachers of English (NCTE) Annual Convention in St. Louis, Missouri. I was fortunate to participate in a panel titled "The Secret of Crafting Engaging Nonfiction" with two of the most talented children's nonfiction authors of our time—Candace Fleming and Deborah Heiligman.

Candace Fleming, Alyson Beecher, Deborah Heiligman, and Melissa Stewart at the 2017 NCTE Annual Convention.

During our discussion, which was moderated by educator and children's nonfiction enthusiast Alyson Beecher, we dove deeply into what fuels our work and why we routinely dedicate years of our lives to a single manuscript. As we compared our thoughts and experiences, we came to realize something critically important—each of our books has a piece of us at its heart. And that personal connection is what drives us to keep working despite the inevitable obstacles and setbacks.

Several other nonfiction authors attended our presentation, and afterward they praised our insights. That conversation helped us all understand our creative process in a new and exciting way.

Because I wanted to share this new-found knowledge with teachers and students, I developed a writing workshop to help young writers enrich their prose by adding a piece of themselves. The initial results were phenomenal. When students in grades 4–8 spent time analyzing and synthesizing their research, they were able to make meaningful connections, which allowed them to present the material in unique and interesting ways.

Around the same time, Laura Purdie Salas, one of the authors who attended our NCTE presentation, contributed to a post titled "Nonfiction Books and the Creative Process (Part 1)" on the Lerner Publishing Group's blog (Hinz, n.d.). In this piece, Laura bravely described how her childhood feelings of embarrassment and shame about her family's strict rules and unusual behavior motivated her to write *Meet My Family! Animal Babies and Their Families*. I was so intrigued by Laura's comments that I invited her to write a more expansive essay on this topic for my blog, *Celebrate Science*.

Because Laura's post, "Nonfiction Authors Aren't Robots," was a huge hit and my student workshop was working so well, I wanted to explore how nonfiction authors are personally connected to their work even more deeply. I decided to host a yearlong blog series in which a wide variety of award-winning authors discussed this topic from their point of view. The results were amazing. Not only did each writer have something uniquely fascinating to say, but many of the contributors also reported learning something valuable about themselves and their creative process while writing their essay.

After I'd published about a dozen of these blog posts, educators began suggesting that I compile them all in one place so that they'd be easier to access and explore as a group. They also asked for teaching strategies to help students approach nonfiction writing in a similar way. Those requests eventually led to this book. Because an NCTE panel played such a pivotal role in developing the ideas presented here, it's deeply satisfying that NCTE is our publisher.

How to Use This Book

Thirty-eight of the mentor essays included in this book are adapted and updated from the posts that appeared on my blog during the 2018–19 school year. The rest were written more recently to help round out the collection.

We have no doubt that the essays can be used in a variety of ways to enrich K–12 nonfiction reading and writing instruction, and we encourage educators to integrate them into their lesson plans in whatever way makes sense to them. For example, some of the essays can serve as mentor texts as students write personal narratives. Others can be used to model the spirit of inquiry. We'd love to hear your creative ideas for integrating the essays into your curriculum. Feel free to tag us on social media and let us know how our ideas have inspired you. Nothing makes us happier than hearing that we're helping educators develop more powerful pedagogy.

The specific focus of this book is helping

Defining Nonfiction

Different people define the term *nonfiction* in different ways. In this book, we've adopted a broad definition, which includes expository nonfiction/informational writing, narrative nonfiction, memoir, graphic/comics nonfiction, fact-based poetry, and fact-based pseudonarratives (Englert & Hiebert, 1984). We chose this wide-ranging definition because it represents the spectrum of children's books available to you and your students and because the writers of these books all engage in the kind of prewriting process we're interested in sharing with educators.

educators who work with students in grades 4–8 gain a stronger understanding of three steps in the prewriting process that don't seem to get enough attention in most classrooms—choosing a topic (Chapter 1), finding a focus (Chapter 2), and making a personal connection (Chapter 3). By providing a sneak peek into how professional nonfiction writers think and how they work, the mentor essays offer insights that will empower you to teach these important aspects of nonfiction writing more effectively.

A Note on Organization

Each of the three chapters in this book is divided into three parts, as shown in Figure 1. A section that includes sixteen or seventeen essays by mentor authors is sandwiched between a Getting Started section that provides helpful background information and an In the Classroom section that suggests tools, tips, teaching strategies, and activities to help you put the ideas discussed in the essays into practice.

It's important to note that while the mentor essays have been sorted into three groups, many of them could have been placed in one or both of the other categories. The location of each essay is based on which step in the prewriting process it seems to focus on most.

Please also note that the mentor essays are snapshots. They reflect each author's thinking on a particular day about a particular book or group of books. To help you and your students get a sense of how a writer's work style varies over time, and based on the demands of different books, I have included a variety of personal experiences in the Getting Started and In the Classroom sections.

FIGURE 1. Organization of chapters

These anecdotes are meant to broaden the presentation and provide additional insights into the prewriting processes of professional writers.

Although it may seem like the three steps we're focusing on—choosing a topic, finding a focus, and making a personal connection—are distinct and should occur in a specific order, in reality they're interconnected and difficult to tease apart. The truth is that writing is messy, and it's recursive. As you read the essays, you'll discover that sometimes nonfiction writers have a focus in mind before they select a topic. Other times a personal connection inspires a writer to choose a particular topic or focus on a specific theme or concept. And, in fact, in some cases, one or more of these "prewriting" steps may not occur until after a writer has begun drafting their manuscript.

Teacher Timesaver Tables

This book is bursting with ideas and insights from many of today's leading non-fiction authors. Ideally, you'll eventually have a chance to read all the essays. But because time is such a precious commodity, you should feel free to dip in and out of the essays in a way that meets your interests and needs.

To help guide your reading, at the beginning of each Essays by Mentor Authors section you'll find a Teacher Timesaver table with helpful information about the essays and the books each author writes. By consulting this table, you can quickly discover the grade level(s) that each author writes for, the format of their books—picture book (PB) or long form (LF)—and the content area the books address. The table also includes a brief summary of each essay. Here is a sample entry for Chapter 1, which explores how writers choose a topic:

Author	Grade Level	Book Format	Content Area	Essay Highlights
Lita Judge	4–5	PB	STEM	Lita's nonfiction books grow from an exploration of deep and lifelong passions. She chooses topics based on her experiences studying living and extinct animals in the field.

This table will help you identify the best two or three essays for your specific needs as you prepare a lesson. As you read the essays you've selected, think about how the authors' ideas and experiences can enrich your reading and writing instruction.

If your students don't usually think about the people behind the nonfiction books they read, the essays will give your class a chance to hear the authors' voices and understand their motivation for writing particular books.

If you do an author study of one of the writers included in this book, sharing their essay can help your class feel more connected to that person.

If you use books written by these authors as mentor texts in writing workshop, the essays can bring a new dimension to your lessons. By revealing how professional nonfiction writers think, the essays can help demystify the writing process for students.

In some cases, you may wish to share an entire essay with your class. In other cases, you may decide to select a few excerpts that complement or enhance the ideas you're focusing on. And sometimes, the essays may inform and expand your own thinking but don't need to be shared with your class at all. Since no one knows your students better than you do, you should feel free to use the essays in the way that best meets your needs and theirs.

Okay, now that you understand how *Nonfiction Writers Dig Deep* is organized and how you can use it to enrich and invigorate your instruction, let's get started!

Choosing a Topic

Getting Started

When I began doing school visits in 2003, teachers usually asked me to focus on the science content in my books rather than on the nonfiction writing process. But that suddenly changed around 2013 as schools began implementing the Common Core State Standards, which put a new emphasis on informational writing.

As I studied the new standards, I realized that they stressed the importance of craft and structure, so I developed a presentation that looked closely at text features, text structures, point of view, voice, and word choice. But at the end of my session, teachers kept asking me questions about the mechanics of my process—how I revised, how I gathered information, and especially how I chose a topic.

Teachers told me that, in the past, they had assigned topics for nonfiction reports. In many cases, the topics were related to the social studies curriculum. Teachers would pass out a list of historical figures and significant events and expect students to choose one. According to teachers, the resulting writing was often dull and uninspired.

Teachers also told me that their current curriculum suggested asking students to write about "something they could teach" based on the age-old advice to "write what you know." The rationale was that students would be more engaged when they tackled a familiar topic. But once again, the results were lackluster.

I wasn't surprised to hear these stories. After all, why would kids want to choose a topic from a prescribed list? And why would they want to rehash something they already know backward and forward when there's a wide world of ideas and information out there just waiting to be explored?

I write about science because I'm fascinated by the natural world. I'm con-

Doing research for *Seashells: More Than a Home* at Haʻena State Park, Kauai, Hawaii.

stantly encountering things that make me ask questions. And to satisfy my curiosity, I want to know more, more, more. Learning more gets me so excited that I'm dying to share my new knowledge with other people. That's what fuels my writing.

Young writers are no different from me. When students focus on ideas they care about or information that fascinates them, when they conduct research to satisfy their own curiosity, they'll craft nonfiction that sings.

But letting young writers choose their own topics leads to a whole new set of challenges, doesn't it? For some students, coming up with ideas is intimidating, even paralyzing.

For a long time, I didn't truly appreciate the severity of this writing obstacle. But then, during a school visit in Rhode Island in 2017, I had an experience that changed my way of thinking.

As I was presenting to fourth graders, I noticed that the students were having trouble recalling the steps of the nonfiction writing process, so I decided to work with them to list the steps in order on chart paper.

We didn't get very far. Despite giving them every hint I could think of, they couldn't name the first step. They kept saying things like "Write your title." and "Choose your photos." Out of desperation, one boy suggested, "Get a piece of paper." Finally, the school librarian came to my rescue by asking, "What's the hardest part of the whole process?"

Suddenly sixty hands shot into the air. They all knew the answer—choosing a topic.

I was gobsmacked. In this school community, choosing a topic was universally acknowledged as THE most difficult part of writing nonfiction. How could that be? Why was something that's so simple for me so difficult for young writers?

A few days later, I sat at my desk contemplating this disconnect. Did I have strategies for choosing a topic? I couldn't think of any.

As my eyes drifted upward, above my computer screen, I suddenly realized that I was literally staring at the solution. I didn't have a strategy for coming up with ideas, but I did have a tool for keeping track of them—my Idea Board.

For me, ideas are everywhere. They come from books and articles I read, conversations with other people, places I visit, and experiences I have. The hard part isn't getting ideas; it's remembering them when it's time to start working on a new book.

That's why I have an Idea Board in my office. Anytime I have an idea, I write it on a scrap of paper and tack it up there. Some of those ideas lead nowhere, but others turn into books.

Here's an example. While I was writing the book *A Place for Birds*, I read a magazine article with a single sentence that blew my mind:

Hummingbird eyelashes are the smallest feathers in the world.

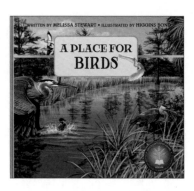

My brain instantly exploded with questions. Birds have eyelashes? And they're made of feathers? Exactly how small are they, and what do they look like?

That incredible fact also inspired me to ask a bigger, broader question: Do birds use their feathers in other unexpected ways? I was dying to find out, but I couldn't let myself get distracted. I had a deadline to meet for *A Place for Birds*.

So I tore the article out of the magazine (*Shh!* It was from the library.) and posted it on my Idea Board along with some related thoughts and questions I didn't want to forget.

As soon as I turned in the manuscript for *A Place for Birds*, I snatched that article off my Idea Board and dove into the research. And eventually, the information I gathered during my journey of discovery turned into the book *Feathers: Not Just for Flying*.

There are three things to take away from this anecdote:

1.   Self-generated ideas are powerful.

2.   It's important to be open to ideas *all* the time.

3.   If writers record ideas as they get them, they'll always have something to write about.

Essays by Mentor Authors

Now that you know a little bit about how I get and keep track of ideas, I encourage you to take a look at what some other authors have to say about choosing topics. After all, there's no single right way to go about this or any other step in the nonfiction writing process. Every writer does things a little bit differently, and that's an important message for students to hear.

If you have time, you may want to read all sixteen essays, but if not, Teacher Timesaver Table 1.1 will help you identify the ones that are of greatest value to you right now.

TEACHER TIMESAVER TABLE 1.1. A Guide to Mentor Essays about Choosing a Topic

Author	Grade Level	Book Format*	Content Area*	Essay Highlights
Lita Judge	4–5	PB	STEM	Lita's nonfiction books grow from an exploration of deep and lifelong passions. She chooses topics based on her experiences studying living and extinct animals in the field.
Patricia Valdez	4–5	PB	Bio/STEM	As a Latina scientist, Patricia has had trouble finding mentors. She chooses to write about people who are good role models for girls interested in science.
Susan Hood	4–5	PB	Bio/Arts, Bio/SS	Susan is passionate about "true stories that are real-life fairy tales." She writes about boys and girls whose grit and grace she admires.
Don Tate	4–6	PB	Bio/Arts, Bio/SS	Don chooses subjects that he feels connected with on a personal level. He says, "When our truths are in alignment, that's a story I feel that I can tell."
Lesa Cline-Ransome	4–6	PB	Bio/Arts, Bio/Sports, Bio/SS	Lesa writes the kind of biographies she longed for as a child. She chooses real people who have persevered despite racism, loss, and adversity.
Mara Rockliff	4–6	PB	Bio/Arts, Bio/SS	Mara feels compelled to write about women who have been left out of history books. She wants to show both boys and girls that "Girls can do anything!"
Teresa Robeson	4–6	PB	Bio/STEM	Teresa highlights people from the past who overcame the struggles she faces today—racism, sexism, and being an immigrant. She hopes learning about these people will help young readers tap into their own inner strength.
Michelle Markel	4–8	PB	Bio/Arts, Bio/SS	Michelle is attracted to rebels and stories of perseverance. Because she wants her biographies "to have a beating heart," she strives to give readers a sense of the subject's humanity, passions, and struggles.
Miranda Paul	4–8	PB	STEM	Miranda wrote *Nine Months* because she couldn't find a book to answer her daughter's questions about pregnancy. Miranda's love for her children kept her inspired during the ten-year writing process.

Continued on next page

(Continued)

Laurie Wallmark	4–8	PB	Bio/STEM	Laurie writes about women in STEM because it combines two of her passions—STEM and equal opportunity for all.
Ray Anthony Shepard	4–8, 5–8, 7–8	PB, LF	Bio/SS	Ray looks for real-life stories that show ways people stood up to racial oppression. His goal is to help young readers understand the past without shame, guilt, or resentment.
Sarah Albee	5–8	LF	SS/STEM	According to Sarah, the best writing stems from who a writer is and what they care about most deeply. Many of her topics trace back to childhood experiences and curiosities.
Mary Kay Carson	5–8	LF	STEM	Mary Kay writes STEM-themed books because science has always helped her make sense of and feel connected to the world. She enjoys tagging along as researchers do their work.
Gail Jarrow	5–8	LF	STEM/SS	Gail describes herself as inquisitive and (politely) nosy. Her curiosity leads her to explore people and topics she doesn't know much about.
Anita Silvey	5–8	LF	Bio/STEM, Bio/SS	Anita chooses subjects who believe in something wholeheartedly and are truly devoted to their work and their cause. She also looks for opportunities to do interesting primary research and conduct interviews.
Steve Sheinkin	6–8	LF	Bio/SS	Steve chooses topics that will make history more appealing and memorable to young readers. He looks for true stories that can be told in a fast-paced, cinematic way.

*Key to Abbreviations
Book Format: PB = picture book, LF = long form
Content Area: Bio = biography, SS = social studies/history, STEM = science/technology/engineering/math

After you've read the essays that seem best suited to your current needs, please turn to the In the Classroom section that begins on page 59. It provides a variety of practical ideas that can help you support students as they choose topics for nonfiction writing assignments.

⑥ Lita Judge

Lita Judge is the author-illustrator of twenty-five fiction and nonfiction books, including *Mary's Monster*, a YA novel about Mary Shelley and the creation of Frankenstein. Her picture books include *Flight School, Born in the Wild, Homes in the Wild, Red Sled,* and *Hoot and Peep*. Lita worked as a geologist and paleontologist before turning to a life of creating art. She lives in Peterborough, New Hampshire. Visit LitaJudge.net for information about her books and for videos on her creative process.

Nonfiction Mentor Texts

Grades 4–5; PB; STEM

Judge, Lita. *Bird Talk: What Birds Are Saying and Why.* New York: Roaring Brook, 2012.

_____. *Born in the Wild: Baby Mammals and Their Parents.* New York: Roaring Brook, 2014.

_____. *Homes in the Wild: Where Baby Animals and Their Parents Live.* New York: Roaring Brook, 2019.

_____. *How Big Were Dinosaurs?* New York: Roaring Brook, 2013.

_____. *Play in the Wild: How Baby Animals Like to Have Fun.* New York: Roaring Brook, 2020.

Exploring Lifelong Passions to Write and Illustrate Nonfiction

As an author and illustrator of both fiction and nonfiction picture books, I'm often startled when someone asks if my fictional books are harder to create and if I turn to nonfiction projects in between as a form of rest. I think this misconception comes from the notion that writing nonfiction picture books entails lightly researching a topic in the library until the writer comes up with a list of facts that make their way into a book.

Many of us were taught to write nonfiction that way in school, but that's not at all how professional nonfiction writers tackle their work. The truth is that my nonfiction books grow from an exploration of deep and lifelong passions. These books are a reflection of who I am. And the research I do to write them goes far beyond the boundaries of a library. It involves time spent in the field, hours of observation, exchanges with scientists, and drawing from nature.

For example, my book *Bird Talk: What Birds Are Saying and Why* explores the ways birds communicate and what their vocal and gestural behaviors mean. This book was inspired by my grandmother, an ornithologist who worked for fifteen years to successfully breed a golden eagle in captivity.

In the predawn hours of a wintery spring, I listened to the piercing call of a golden eagle beckoning my grandmother to her pen. My grandmother rose, dressed quickly, and ran outside carrying sticks to bring as an offering for the eagle to begin building a nest. Later, when eggs were laid, my grandmother and the eagle shared the work of incubating.

I also worked with my grandparents on the marsh, banding owls and hawks,

learning to differentiate the calls between mates locating each other from those that warned of danger or responses to hungry chicks. *Bird Talk* grew from many experiences gained by research in the field.

I've also written about dinosaurs. Like so many other kids, I had a love for dinosaurs. When I was fourteen, I was convinced I wanted to be a paleontologist. In hopes of pursuing this goal, I wrote dozens of letters

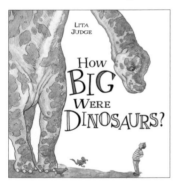

to museums begging to volunteer on a dinosaur dig. After many rejections, at last Phil Currie from the Tyrrell Museum of Paleontology in Alberta, Canada, agreed to let me work on a dig.

I ended up working in the Canadian Badlands for several summers and eventually got a degree in geology, but over time I discovered that I really wanted to write and illustrate books about dinosaurs more than work as a paleontologist. So I turned to writing books, such as *How Big Were Dinosaurs?*, which answers many of the childhood questions I had about dinosaurs.

Sometimes I feel people assume writing nonfiction picture books like *Born in the Wild: Baby Mammals and Their Parents* is simple because of its short text. But it requires a breadth of knowledge to take complex ideas and shape them into understandable concepts for young readers. The best way to gain that knowledge is through countless hours of observing wildlife in its natural habitat. My

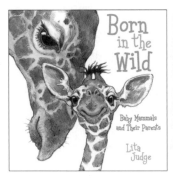  

desire to study the intimate lives of animals inspired two more books: *Homes in the Wild: Where Baby Animals and Their Parents Live* and *Play in the Wild: How Baby Animals Like to Have Fun*.

Research for a book often involves being in the field in direct contact with my subject. I've spent long cold days sitting quietly in a wildlife blind, waiting for a grizzly bear and her cubs to emerge from their winter den. I've watched that same mother show her cubs where squirrels cache their seeds and flip over large rocks to reveal a meal of moths.

By watching through a spotting scope, sketching and carefully recording my observations, I've learned how a wolf pack works together to raise a litter of pups.

And I've volunteered in a research program at a zoo so that I could go behind the scenes to help with breeding programs for endangered animals. There I watched a giraffe give birth and observed cheetah cubs as they played and learned hunting skills.

I create picture books because so much of the knowledge I acquire working in the field is visual. Watching animals gives me an awareness of subtle gestures and body language. I could never do these topics justice if my knowledge of them stemmed only from reading books on the topic. And the time I spend observing animals results in a desire to draw and record my knowledge as illustrations rather than solely write about them. That's why I love the genre of picture books.

◎ Patricia Valdez

Patricia Valdez is a scientist and author of the award-winning picture book biography *Joan Procter, Dragon Doctor*. She earned her PhD in molecular and cell biology from the University of California, Berkeley. Originally from Texas, Patricia now lives in the Washington, DC, area with her husband, children, cats, and turtle, while continuing to write true stories for curious kids. Visit her at patriciavaldezbooks.com.

Nonfiction Mentor Text

Grades 4–5; PB; Bio/STEM

Valdez, Patricia. *Joan Procter, Dragon Doctor: The Woman Who Loved Reptiles.* New York: Knopf, 2018.

A Scientist in Search of Role Models

When asked to imagine a typical scientist, most people picture a man with wild hair, like Albert Einstein, or with a bow tie and lab coat, like Bill Nye.

A peek inside a laboratory today would reveal that, yes, women work in labs, too! That said, women seem to disappear from science as we look farther up the ladder. And the situation for women of color is much worse.

Why is this happening?

The importance of role models and mentors is clear. The limited number of women at the top makes mentors scarce. Sure, men can be great mentors to women, but it's never easy to work in an environment where you are considered "other." Role models show young girls that, yes, they can make it, too.

The more role models, the better.

One of the reasons I write picture book biographies is to shine light on women whose scientific contributions have been ignored or forgotten. Both boys and girls need to know that women have been contributing to scientific discovery since the dawn of man (and woman).

Joan Beauchamp Procter, the subject of my picture book biography, *Joan Procter, Dragon Doctor*, knew from an early age that she would devote her life to the study of reptiles. She found a great mentor in George Boulenger, curator at London's Natural History Museum. He realized her genius early on.

When Boulenger retired, Joan took over as curator, but many of the men were uncomfortable with a woman in charge. To them, Joan was "other." They wanted to hire a less-qualified man to supervise Joan, so she took another job at the London Zoo in 1923.

Joan Procter regularly challenged people's presumptions about what women could or should be. When interviewed by newspaper reporters, she often insisted that they focus on the animals and not her gender. "Why shouldn't a woman run a reptile house?" she asked. Still, the newspaper headlines always managed to sneak words like *girl* or *lady* into the headline.

Joan even challenged people's presumptions about the animals under her care. She presented papers that dispelled myths about the size and temperament of Komodo dragons. Perhaps Joan felt a deep connection with Komodo dragons because, like her, they were misunderstood in a world that considered them "other."

As a Latina scientist, I've often been in situations where I might be considered "other." I've had difficulty finding good mentors throughout my career. I hope someday that women and people of color will occupy more rungs at the top of the ladder.

To paraphrase Joan Procter: *Why shouldn't a woman run the world?*

⊚ Susan Hood

Susan Hood is the recipient of the E. B. White Read Aloud Picture Book Honor, the Christopher Award, and the Flora Stieglitz Straus Award, given to "a distinguished work of nonfiction that serves as an inspiration to young people." When not writing, Susan enjoys sailing with her husband and is all too familiar with trouble at sea. Those experiences informed Susan's middle grade book—*Lifeboat 12*, based on a true World War II story discovered in family letters. Visit Susan at susanhoodbooks.com.

Nonfiction Mentor Texts

Grades 4–5; PB; Bio/Arts; Bio/SS

Hood, Susan. *Ada's Violin: The Story of the Recycled Orchestra of Paraguay.* New York: Simon & Schuster, 2016.

_____. *Shaking Things Up: 14 Young Women Who Changed the World.* New York: HarperCollins, 2018.

_____, and Pathana Sornhiran. *Titan and the Wild Boars: The True Cave Rescue of the Thai Soccer Team.* New York: HarperCollins, 2019.

Whiz Kids, Underdogs, and Real-Life Fairy Tales

One day I saw this necklace on Etsy and knew I had to have it.

Those who know their Dewey Decimal System will know it says, "I still believe in fairy tales." And I do. Not the insipid Sleeping Beauty/Prince Charm-ing movies I grew up with, but the stories that terrified and fascinated me as a young reader. They told me flat out what I already suspected—that the world can be a scary place, but kids (boys *and girls*) can succeed. Gretel can outsmart the wicked witch, save her brother, and find the way out of the forest.

What does a childhood love of fairy tales have to do with writing nonfiction?

Today I'm passionate about true stories that are real-life fairy tales. I want to write about boys and girls whose grit and grace knock my socks off.

Take young Ada Ríos, who grew up on a landfill in Paraguay, learned to play musical instruments made from recycled trash, became a first violinist in the Recycled Orchestra, and now plays for the IPU Paraguay Philharmonic Orchestra. The story behind *Ada's Violin: The Story of the Recycled Orchestra of Paraguay* (illustrated by Sally Wern Comport) is a fairy tale if ever I heard one, but it's TRUE.

Thanks to growing up on fairy tales, I'm inspired by underdogs and their pursuit of happiness. I want to write about young people who have no magic wand, no fairy godmother, and yet persevere in the face of adversity. *Shaking Things Up: 14 Young Women Who Changed the World*, with art by thirteen extraordinary women illustrators, came about because of a series of events in 2016—a perfect storm.

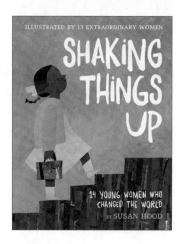

My first grandchild—a granddaughter—was born at a time when prominent women were being interrupted, mansplained, or silenced; all the advances women had made over the decades seemed in danger of backsliding. As author Frances Moore Lappé wrote, "Every choice we make can be a celebration of the world we want." So I decided to write about fourteen young women who faced poverty, illness, discrimination, or war head-on to pursue their interests and talents.

There's thirteen-year-old Mary Anning, who sold fossils to keep her family from starving and discovered an ichthyosaur. She split scientific theory wide open, providing evidence of extinction and evolution forty-seven years before Charles Darwin published *On the Origin of Species*.

I was lucky enough to meet Ruby Bridges, who in first grade marched through a screaming throng at an all-white school in New Orleans and became an icon of the Civil Rights Movement. Her bravery—at age six!—astounded me.

Perhaps nothing was more astounding than the true-life fairy tale that riveted the world in the summer of 2018—the heart-breaking report of twelve soccer players and their young coach trapped inside a flooding cave in Thailand.

In a rare, stunning example of international cooperation, twenty-three countries rushed to their rescue. However, when I interviewed two of the four lead divers, they admitted that none of them thought the boys would survive. The

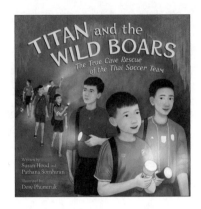

pitch-black cave was too long, too narrow, too treacherous even for the best divers in the world.

The death of triathlete and Thai Navy SEAL Saman Kunan confirmed their worst fears. And yet these courageous divers couldn't give up; they had to *try* to get the boys out. After eighteen grueling days, thanks to the teamwork of both the boys and the rescuers, they pulled off the impossible. All thirteen members of the team were saved! *Titan and the Wild Boars: The True Cave Rescue of the Thai Soccer Team*, coauthored with Thai journalist Pathana Sornhiran, who reported outside the cave during the ordeal, and illustrated by Dow Phumiruk, is the story I still can't believe is true. But it is.

Kids today are bombarded with news 24/7; they are more aware than ever that the world can be a scary place. Children's books can provide context, explain different points of view, encourage kindness and empathy, provide hope, inspire, and empower young readers. Kids like Ada Ríos, Mary Anning, Ruby Bridges, and Titan and the Wild Boars really can change the world. And that ain't no fairy tale.

⊚ Don Tate

Don Tate is an award-winning author and the illustrator of numerous critically acclaimed books for children. He is also one of the founding hosts of *The Brown Bookshelf*, a blog designed to push awareness of the myriad African American voices writing for young readers that includes book reviews and author and illustrator interviews. Don lives in Austin, Texas.

Nonfiction Mentor Texts

Grades 4–6; PB; Bio/Arts; Bio/SS

Tate, Don. *It Jes' Happened: When Bill Traylor Started to Draw.* New York: Lee & Low, 2012.

_____. *Poet: The Remarkable Story of George Moses Horton.* Atlanta, GA: Peachtree, 2015.

_____. *Strong as Sandow: How Eugen Sandow Became the Strongest Man on Earth.* Watertown, MA: Charlesbridge, 2017.

The Picture Book Biography: Connecting Inner Truths

When I first got into publishing and for many years afterward, I avoided the topic of slavery, so it's interesting to me that with my first two authored books, I took on the topic.

It Jes' Happened: When Bill Traylor Started to Draw is the biography of once enslaved outsider artist Bill Traylor who, with no prior art training, created a body of artwork that is celebrated and collected around the world today.

Poet: The Remarkable Story of George Moses Horton is the story of an enslaved poet who became the first African American to get a book published in the South. His poetry protested his enslavement.

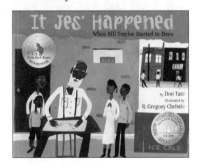

Why did I decide to write these books? When I was a child in school, the horrors of slavery weren't addressed very much in the classroom, and movies misrepresented—and sometimes even glamorized—the topic. As a result, I grew up misinformed and even ashamed of the subject. Through research, I learned how African Americans fought for and overcame tremendous adversity to obtain the rights we enjoy today. I realized the importance of preserving these stories and sharing them with children.

Researching the life of Bill Traylor presented a challenge. Traylor couldn't read or write; therefore, he left no written records of his life. But he did leave behind something invaluable—his artwork, pictures he drew on the back of trash. They helped to fill in the missing pieces of his life. His drawings depict his life as an enslaved man, his later life as a free sharecropper, and the years he spent on the streets of Montgomery, Alabama, as a homeless artist.

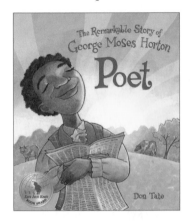

The topic of literacy and the importance of reading is what drew me to George Moses Horton's story. As an enslaved child, Horton wasn't allowed to learn how to read. But he taught himself by listening to his master's children when they studied books. While Horton spent the majority of his life enslaved, becoming literate allowed him to earn enough money as a poet to live as a full-time writer on a college campus.

Set during slavery years, *Poet* presented some of the same challenges as *It Jes' Happened*. Primary sources were scarce. But once again, by researching art—Horton's poetry —I found my answers. Horton's poetry allowed me to get inside his head, to understand his feelings about his circumstances as a slave and how he viewed the world and people around him.

For my third authored book, *Strong as Sandow: How Eugen Sandow Became the Strongest Man on Earth*, I tapped into a different part of who I am.

I love physical fitness activities. Throughout the years, I've run, swum, worked out with weights, practiced yoga. After winning trophies in natural bodybuilding contests twenty years ago, I wanted to write a book on the subject.

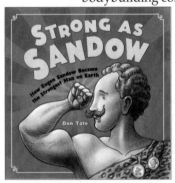

Victorian bodybuilder Eugen Sandow was the perfect way into that world.

I had many more sources to rely on in telling Sandow's story, but there were still unique challenges. After Sandow died, his wife and daughters burned all of his belongings! Needless to say, they weren't interested in preserving his legacy. But that's another story.

Because of Sandow's huge celebrity status, he'd been well interviewed and written about. He was also the best-selling author of the Victorian physical fitness bible, *Strength and How to Obtain It*. A short autobiography was squeezed into the center of the book.

Another challenge with researching Sandow's life was his over-the-top telling of his own story. Sandow was a professional strongman. But first and foremost, he was a gifted showman. He was selling a product—himself.

Honestly, I think a lot of what sold was hyperbole and illusion. I mean, did he really hoist a grand piano over his head, with a full orchestra and a large dog on top? Did he really wrestle a 500-pound lion? Well, yes, and maybe yes. These things were documented by reporters and news outlets of the time. But no doubt, there was some trickery at play. I wrote a story that I believed Eugen Sandow would have wanted told based on my research of his life—puny kid who grew up to be known as the "Strongest Man on Earth."

In my thirty-plus year career, I've written and/or illustrated more than fifty books. Most have been nonfiction. With each one, I study my subject's life, trying to understand their inner truth. I need to know what makes them tick. But I also consider what makes me tick—my inner truth. When our truths are in alignment, that's a story I feel that I can tell.

⊚ Lesa Cline-Ransome

Lesa Cline-Ransome is the author of nearly twenty books for children, including *Light in the Darkness: A Story about How Slaves Learned in Secret* and *Freedom's School*. *Before She Was Harriet* received a Christopher Award, a Jane Addams Children's Book Honor Award, and a Coretta Scott King Honor Award for Illustration. Lesa's middle grade novel *Finding Langston* received the 2019 Scott O'Dell Award for Historical Fiction. She lives with her husband and frequent collaborator, illustrator James Ransome. Visit her at www.lesacline ransome.com.

Nonfiction Mentor Texts

Grades 4–6; PB; Bio/Arts, Bio/Sports, Bio/SS

Cline-Ransome, Lesa. *Before She Was Harriet.* New York: Holiday House, 2017.

_____. *Just a Lucky So and So: The Story of Louis Armstrong.* New York: Holiday House, 2016.

_____. *Major Taylor, Champion Cyclist.* New York: Simon & Schuster/Atheneum, 2004.

_____. *My Story, My Dance: Robert Battle's Journey to Alvin Ailey.* New York: Simon & Schuster/Paula Wiseman, 2015.

_____. *Satchel Paige.* New York: Simon & Schuster, 2000.

_____. *Words Set Me Free: The Story of Young Frederick Douglass.* New York: Simon & Schuster/Paula Wiseman, 2012.

_____. *Young Pelé: Soccer's First Star.* New York: Schwartz & Wade, 2007.

Facing Our Past, Healing Our Future

Much of my life has been shaped by stories. From my earliest days, as a visitor to the Malden Public Library in Massachusetts, I was transformed by the stories I read.

As a young girl, so shy and nervous I was often too afraid to speak, I devoured the fictional stories of fearless girls and rabble-rousers. In them, I saw a seedling of myself, waiting to take root.

Yet, while I read stories by Astrid Lindgren and Judy Blume, I avoided biographies. The often bland, didactic narratives of seemingly perfect people with perfect lives failed to resonate with me in the way that fictional characters could.

Instead of seeing inspiration and potential, I saw a failure in myself to reach the level of perfectionism required to be successful. Where was the grit and perseverance and fierce independence of a girl like Pippi Longstocking, orphaned, living alone, fending off all manner of danger? The divide between fiction and nonfiction was vast in my eyes—that is, until I read the story of Harriet Tubman.

As the only Black student in a classroom of all whites, I dreaded the time of year when slavery was discussed. The room would grow uncomfortably quiet as my classmates stole glances in my direction because they felt that, somehow, those inaccurate and incomplete descriptions of enslaved persons portrayed the complete sum of my African American ancestry. In my history, they saw people too weak, too afraid, too incapable of resisting bondage.

But then, one year, we read about Harriet Tubman. Her story was like one of an action adventure hero, complete with danger, disguise, late night plots, and daring escape. Because her story was also true, it was even better than the adventures of Pippi Longstocking.

Harriet suffered at the hands of slave masters, was unschooled, and endured persistent health problems. She was rejected by her husband when she returned to rescue him. Yet despite these impediments, she kept right on striving.

Now this, I thought, was a real-life hero.

I realized then that it wasn't that I disliked biographies. What I disliked were the biographies I'd been handed in the past. I needed to read stories about people who looked like me. People who had persevered despite racism, loss, and adversity.

When I began writing for children, I wrote the kind of biographies I longed for as a child. My earliest books included *Satchel Paige*; *Young Pelé: Soccer's First Star*; and *Major Taylor, Champion Cyclist*. You won't find these athletes' names in social studies textbooks, alongside names such as Babe Ruth and Joe DiMaggio. Their stories of struggling to reach their potential against all odds drew me in. Their stories are human stories of how small ripples can cause big waves in the fight for dignity and equal access.

Books like *Just a Lucky So and So: The Story of Louis Armstrong* and *My Story, My Dance: Robert Battle's Journey to Alvin Ailey* seek to highlight the role of the African American influence on the arts.

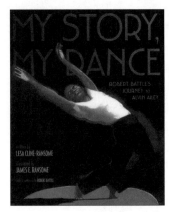

Diving further into history with the biography of Frederick Douglass in *Words Set Me Free* helped me discover one young boy's quest for dignity and freedom in the form of education. And as I told the story of Harriet Tubman in *Before She Was Harriet*, I remembered how all those years ago her story of courage gave me hope that I too could one day be fearless.

These true stories reveal the crucial role of African Americans in the building of this country and how the lessons from a troubled history can provide a road map to a bet-  ter future. They give young readers a broader understanding of our shared history, our culture, and our strengths.

I still love Pippi Longstocking, but in each of the figures I've written about, I found the real-life stories of fearlessness I sought as a young girl. And ultimately, both off and on the page, I found my voice.

 Mara Rockliff

Mara Rockliff is the author of many lively historical picture books, including Cook Prize winner *Mesmerized: How Ben Franklin Solved a Mystery That Baffled All of France*, illustrated by Iacopo Bruno, and *Doctor Esperanto and the Language of Hope*, illustrated by Zosia Dzierzawska. Here she is baking gingerbread for her book *Gingerbread for Liberty! How a German Baker Helped Win the American Revolution*, illustrated by Vincent X. Kirsch. Visit her online at mararockliff.com.

Nonfiction Mentor Texts

Grades 4–6; PB; Bio/Arts, Bio/SS

Rockliff, Mara. *Anything but Ordinary Addie: The True Story of Adelaide Herrmann, Queen of Magic*. Somerville, MA: Candlewick, 2016.

_____. *Born to Swing: Lil Hardin Armstrong's Life in Jazz*. Honesdale, PA: Calkins Creek, 2018.

_____. *Lights! Camera! Alice! The Thrilling True Adventures of the First Woman Filmmaker*. San Francisco: Chronicle, 2018.

The Heroines Our Children Need

When my daughter was ten, I brought home an award-winning documentary about a high school jazz band competition. My daughter played trumpet, and I thought she'd be inspired seeing older students play. Instead, I watched her face fall as we both slowly realized that the filmmakers had totally excluded girls. Only boys were interviewed; when a band played, the camera cut away from girls and focused on the boys. In our town, school bands had at least as many girls as boys. But in this film, girls who played jazz simply did not exist.

That film failed to inspire my daughter, but it did inspire me—to dig into jazz history and write *Born to Swing: Lil Hardin Armstrong's Life in Jazz*.

Lil was an amazing pioneer. At a time when jazz bands hired women only as "canaries" (singers), she pounded the piano for the hottest jazz band in Chicago.

She was a composer, too, who wrote and arranged hit songs such as "Brown Gal" and "Just for a Thrill." And it was Lil's sophistication, influence, and drive that turned her husband, Louis Armstrong, from an unknown trumpet player into a legend of jazz.

The musicians who played with Lil (and for her—she was a bandleader, too!) spoke of her with admiration and respect. But when the history of jazz was written, Lil became a footnote to her famous husband. No one seemed to care about her own remarkable career.

Our kids *need* Lil Hardin Armstrong. Girls learning to play an instrument need to know that they belong, that they've always belonged, that before there was a Miles or a Charlie or a Dizzy, there was Lil. And boys need to know, too, so they don't grow into men who make a movie that erases girls.

Speaking of making movies, our children also need to know the story of Alice Guy-Blaché, star of *Lights! Camera! Alice! The Thrilling True Adventures of the First Woman Filmmaker*.

Alice was not only the first woman filmmaker, but also one of the very first filmmakers, period. Decades before the first Hollywood talkies and Technicolor, she made movies that had sound and color, as well as special effects.

To make her movies more exciting, Alice would blow up a pirate ship or crawl into a cage with a tiger. She convinced her actresses to jump from bridges onto moving trains. She tied up an actor, smeared the ropes with food, and sent in live rats to gnaw him free.

Alice Guy-Blaché was a celebrity. But once again, when the first film histories were written, Alice's name disappeared. Credit for her films went to her male assistants, or even to men she'd never met, men who had never directed a film. So unfair—not just to Alice but to all the girls who never knew they could

make movies, too. Our kids *need* Alice Guy-Blaché because, for every woman directing a major feature film in Hollywood today, there are still not two, not three, but TWENTY-TWO men.

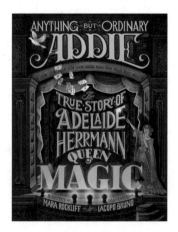

And why are there so few women magicians? Maybe it's because generations of kids have grown up reading about Harry Houdini, the Handcuff King, while the Queen of Magic who preceded him has vanished—*poof!*—from our collective memory. She reappears in *Anything but Ordinary Addie: The True Story of Adelaide Herrmann, Queen of Magic*.

Addie was a superstar. Like Lil and Alice, she was strong, hardworking, capable, adventurous, fun-loving, and full of personality. (Unlike them, she could make candies rain down from the sky and catch a fired bullet on a china plate.) Addie made it to the top, even though she had to do it, as they say, "backward and in high heels." Our kids *need* Addie Herrmann because girls love magic just as much as boys.

We can tell our kids "Girls can do anything!" but we also need to show them how much women have already done. Children need heroines like Alice, Lil, and Addie, because when women are written out of history, we're written out of the present and future, too.

⊚ Teresa Robeson

Teresa Robeson was born in Hong Kong, raised in Canada, and now lives on a mini-homestead in southern Indiana with her scientist husband. She draws on her Chinese heritage, Canadian American sensibilities, and her background in science and love of nature when she writes. A nonfiction winner of the We Need Diverse Books mentorship program, Teresa advocates for greater scientific and cultural literacy. *Queen of Physics*, a biography that won the 2020 APALA Literature Award in the Picture Book Category, was her debut. Find her at http://teresarobeson.com.

Nonfiction Mentor Text

Grades 4–6; PB; Bio/STEM

Robeson, Teresa. *Queen of Physics: How Wu Chien Shiung Helped Unlock the Secrets of the Atom.* New York: Sterling, 2019.

Confronting Challenges through Nonfiction

The stories I tell are sculpted and informed by the struggles I face: against racism, being an immigrant and a visible minority; against sexism; and against my own lack of self-confidence, which prevents me from achieving goals I am capable of. As draining as they are, these personal challenges guide me as a writer. The struggles I face lead me to seek out people from the past who encountered similar adversities and triumphed over them.

Because these individuals inspire me, I know they can serve as examples for others. It is my hope that by learning about the travails of those who have gone before them, young readers can tap into their own inner strength to overcome obstacles or explore options that they previously thought were closed to them.

Due to my lifelong love of math and science, I also find myself being drawn to people who worked in those areas. While I admire anyone who breaks race and gender barriers, my heart beats a little faster if they are also mathematicians or scientists.

This is why I felt compelled to write *Queen of Physics*, a picture book biography of Wu Chien Shiung. As an immigrant from China, Wu refused to let the racism and sexism of the 1940s and 1950s deter her. She worked twice as hard as her colleagues, pushed boundaries, spoke up when she needed to, and became a prominent scientist in her field, achieving many firsts for Asians and for women. I want her story to embolden girls and marginalized kids to stare down the naysayers and blaze their own trails. I want her story to embolden *me*.

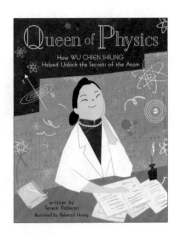

Driven by the need to overcome my personal struggles, plus the desire to share my passion for STEM, I continue to work on biographies of people who move me. I'm drawn to women who were notable in their fields but are not household names, as their male counterparts are. I also have an affinity for minorities who have made important discoveries while enduring patronizing dismissals from their colleagues. I may lack the self-confidence to sing my own praises, but I am dedicated to raising awareness about those who had to fight hard to make their mark on the world.

But my writing is not always about the struggles. Sometimes passion gets the spotlight. I may be in my fifties, but I have a child's sense of wonder. I can often be found examining caterpillars that cross my path or pulling out reference books to look up everything from the taxonomy of dinosaurs to the chain of decay of radioactive isotopes. My yearning to learn naturally lends itself to writing about topics under the wide umbrella of science.

I write about astronomy because I've been an amateur astronomer for forty years. I write about climate change because I studied climatology at university and my husband is a climatologist. I write about ornithology because I've been a birder since my early twenties. I write about ecology and evolution because my whole family is interested in those topics (in fact, my older child is now pursuing a PhD with a focus on both).

If I am honest with myself, though, I will admit that my personal challenges are hidden in my passions. Researching and writing about these topics reassure me that I know more than I give myself credit for. The internal critic that told me I wasn't good enough to go to graduate school for astrophysics was wrong.

Regardless of the motivation, it all works out. I may not be a scientist like my twelve-year-old self wanted to be, but I get to write about science and the accomplishments of women and minorities. And if my books inspire even one child to reach for greater heights, then all my struggles are worth it.

@ Michelle Markel

Michelle Markel is the author of several acclaimed nonfiction picture books, including *The Fantastic Jungles of Henri Rousseau* (PEN/Steven Kroll Award for Picture Book Writing), *Brave Girl: Clara and the Shirtwaist Makers' Strike of 1909* (Jane Addams Children's Book Award; Flora Stieglitz Straus Award; Orbis Pictus Honor Book), and *Balderdash! John Newbery and the Boisterous Birth of Children's Books* (sixteen state awards). She has been an instructor at UCLA Extension's Writers' Program, a teacher, and a freelance writer. Visit her website at www.michellemarkel.com.

Nonfiction Mentor Texts

Grades 4–8; PB; Bio/Arts, Bio/SS

Markel, Michelle. *Brave Girl: Clara and the Shirtwaist Makers' Strike of 1909.* New York: HarperCollins/Balzer + Bray, 2013.

_____. *The Fantastic Jungles of Henri Rousseau.* Grand Rapids, MI: Eerdmans, 2012.

_____. *Out of This World: The Surreal Art of Leonora Carrington.* New York: HarperCollins/Balzer + Bray, 2019.

Nonfiction Stories Have Feelings Too

The picture book biographies of my youth were bloodless recitations of facts. Many years later, when I started writing for children, a new type of illustrated bio was becoming popular: expressive, artistic, poetic. I wanted to write one, too!

It took a while to figure out how to do it. I sold one biography, then suffered rejections for several years. I was going through the dark night of the soul. Then I met Henri Rousseau. Preparing an art program for kids, I came across his "Sleeping Gypsy."

I'd seen the painting before, but this time it spoke to me: the mysterious figure, the moonlit desert, the sweet plush lion that reminded me of a stuffed toy I'd had as a child.

I read up on the artist and learned that he refused to be crushed by the snarky art critics who publicly ridiculed him year after year. Besides painting and exhibiting, Henri gave music lessons to children in the neighborhood, wrote plays, and threw concerts in his little apartment. I felt a great sympathy and admiration for him. I believed kids would feel the same way and thought they'd enjoy his whimsical jungle pictures.

I studied Henri's paintings of cavorting apes and monkeys and imaginary plants. I read his letters and the books written by his friends. And the coolest thing happened. As I worked on that manuscript, the artist's playful, rule-breaking spirit cheered me on. He helped me free up my inhibitions, loosen up my sentences, and find my voice as a nonfiction author. Henri turned my career around. *The Fantastic Jungles of Henri Rousseau* won the 2013 PEN/Steven Kroll Award for Picture Book Writing.

I'm attracted to stories of perseverance. I was drawn to Clara Lemlich, a lifelong labor activist, for a few reasons. Clara came to America from Eastern Europe, as did my grandparents, and, like my father (a former airline mechanic and president of his machinist union), Clara was an advocate for workers' rights.

The story of Clara's role in the Shirtwaist Makers' Strike of 1909 is highly dramatic. Reading the details about the strike brought me to tears—how the immigrant garment workers, many in their teens, fought for humane conditions in the factories; how they stood up to hunger, cold, beatings, and arrests by police and company thugs. I felt an obligation to write this story, even though I had serious doubts that I'd sell it (there are few picture books about feminist labor history).

In the book, I describe how Clara's bravery empowered the other garment workers. She empowered my writing, too. In one of her interviews, Clara said that back then "she had fire in her veins." That fire spread into *Brave Girl*.

Out of This World: The Surreal Art of Leonora Carrington is about another type of rebel. Leonora's otherworldly pictures feature mythical beasts and empowered females—a giantess, women who can grow little trees on their heads and float through ceilings.

Defying societal norms for her class and gender, Leonora moved to Paris to be an artist among the Surrealists. Though my background is quite different from hers (she came from an upper-class British family), I relate to Leonora. As a little girl, I was crazy about fairy tales, too.

I loved reading about Leonora's friendship with the Spanish artist Remedios Varo, whom she met in Mexico after fleeing the Nazis. The two of them were kindred spirits, cooking up stories and strange concoctions, dressing in costumes,

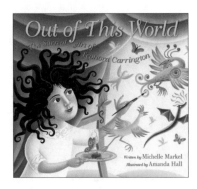

dreaming up their own magic spells and remedies. Their sisterhood reminded me of the joy and emotional support I've gotten from my creative women friends.

Leonora inspired illustrator Amanda Hall and me to take our own risk and submit this book as a joint project—which you're not supposed to do. We were thrilled to find a publisher.

Fine literature is about the human experience, and picture book biographies are no exception. The best of them give a sense of the subject's humanity, of their inner life, passions, and struggles. I want my nonfiction stories to have a beating heart! To write them, I've got to be emotionally involved.

⊚ Miranda Paul

Miranda Paul is the award-winning author of more than a dozen books for children, including *One Plastic Bag, Water Is Water, Whose Hands Are These?, I Am Farmer,* and *Little Libraries, Big Heroes.* Her book *Nine Months* was named a Boston Globe–Horn Book Honor title for nonfiction. Miranda is a cofounding member of the nonprofit We Need Diverse Books and created the organization's mentorship program. She lives with her family in Wisconsin.

Nonfiction Mentor Text

Grades 4–8; PB; STEM

Paul, Miranda. *Nine Months: Before a Baby Is Born*. New York: Holiday House, 2019.

A True Book Baby: The Ten-Year Gestation of Nine Months

My maternal grandmother gave birth seven times and helped take care of fourteen foster babies. One of her sisters had sixteen kids. During a family reunion, I remember relatives hiring a photographer to climb on an industrial ladder so we could all fit in the panorama.

Knowing this, it's not surprising that my mother became the neighborhood babysitter.

Despite all the babies that came into my childhood, knowledge of what an unborn baby looks like remained a mystery. Virtually none of the grown-ups I knew ever discussed the month-by-month science of a developing baby. I grew up believing that pregnancy was something we shouldn't talk about, even though babies seemed to be wildly celebrated.

My childhood public library had lots of books about babies, but the illustrations were mostly clip-art style—a bald, peach baby with a single lock of curly hair. And while our upper-elementary school curriculum made sure we had "the talk" about puberty and (briefly) how babies are made, the actual science of our own development before birth went undiscussed.

Looking back, this seems absurd, since being born is a shared experience of every single human in the world.

It wasn't until I took an optional advanced biology course in high school that I learned my peers and I once had tails! I remember Ms. Hollenback revealing that an embryo's rate of growth is so high during one stage that, if we didn't slow down, humans would give birth to babies as big as an oversized pair of elephants.* Ms. Hollenback's lecture style may have left something to be desired, but the facts themselves were so interesting that I retain many to this day.

Anticipating the arrival of my first child, I signed up for emails that chronicled my baby's development. The more I discovered about the science, the greater my excitement and anticipation. Although I didn't want to know everything—we kept the sex a surprise—I knew when the baby would be able to hear me, when its eyelashes and fingernails would form, and how fast its heartbeat was. When my daughter was finally born, I held her seven-pound body and kissed her full-of-hair head. An entirely new person had grown deep inside me.

Incredible.

With child number two, I reread some of the books and signed up for the emails. But my two-year-old daughter's questions allowed me to realize that there still weren't many books for little ones about fetal development. The book I wanted for her—a short nonfiction text with warm, scientifically accurate illustrations—didn't exist. (Or, if it did, I couldn't find it.) I was transported back to my college days, when my professor, children's book author Lucille Clifton, talked about making a book if it didn't exist, thereby allowing all kids to be seen.

This ignited my dream of creating a children's book that was scientific yet warm, accurate yet appropriate. The accessible text with straightforward facts would reflect our interracial family, in which babies aren't born bald.

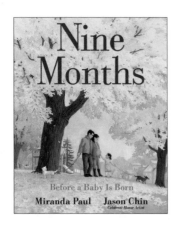

It took me five or six years to research the book and find the right format. (At first I was certain the text shouldn't rhyme.) Over the next two years, I wrote and revised the version of *Nine Months: Before a Baby Is Born* that was submitted to my editor. And more than three years after that, it finally had its own book birthday.

When families read *Nine Months*, I doubt they'll know how deeply this book mirrors my family's experience. Do they notice the interracial couple, based on illustrator Jason Chin's own brother and sister-in-law, who are Chinese American and

---

*I wasn't able to verify this fact while writing *Nine Months*. Instead, the back matter compares a four-year-old to the height of a forty-two-story skyscraper—demonstrating what it would look like to grow like an embryo and become 200 times bigger in a short space of time.

Mexican American respectively? Do they pause at the significance of the doctor's brown hands, holding a healthy baby who is crying and coated with a real-to-life protective layer?

It has been a joy to visit schools and watch kindergartners break into applause at all the things they could do before they were born. The children see themselves on the page, and, in some cases, they react—like the girl who shouted out, unprompted, "Science is so cool! And that means *I* am cool!"

That's the power of a book.

And I'm proud to be its mama.

ⓢ Laurie Wallmark

Award-winning author Laurie Wallmark's women in STEM picture book biographies have received numerous starred reviews and many national awards, including NSTA Outstanding Science Trade Book and Cook Prize Honor Book. Laurie has an MFA from the Vermont College of Fine Arts and taught computer science. Find Laurie at www.lauriewallmark.com and @lauriewallmark.

Nonfiction Mentor Texts

Grades 4–8; PB; Bio/STEM

Wallmark, Laurie. *Ada Byron Lovelace and the Thinking Machine.* Berkeley, CA: Creston, 2015.

_____. *Grace Hopper: Queen of Computer Code.* New York: Sterling, 2017.

_____. *Hedy Lamarr's Double Life: Hollywood Legend and Brilliant Inventor.* New York: Sterling, 2019.

Write Your Passion

Writers are often told to write what they know. As far as I'm concerned, we should write what we're passionate about. We can always research (and who doesn't like research?) a topic, but if we're not interested in it—boring!

Which brings me to why I write about women in STEM (science, technology, engineering, math). Doing so lets me combine two of my passions—STEM and equal opportunity for all.

Ever since I was a little girl, I've loved science and math. In college, I majored in biochemistry, which allowed me to take courses in math, physics, biology, chemistry, and, of course, biochemistry. I was in science-nerd heaven.

I also took a few computer courses (there wasn't yet a computer science major) and found a new love—programming. But how could I combine my new and old loves? Much to my delight, I found out there was a profession called scientific programming. Woo-hoo!

After college, I received a master's degree in information systems and worked in programming for many years. Now I teach computer science at my local community college.

But what about my other passion, wanting to provide equal opportunities for everyone regardless of sex, race, religion, sexual orientation, etc.? As a child, I was convinced I could only become a scientist if I changed my name to Marie Curie. After all, she was the only woman scientist I had ever read about. Through my writing today, I can show girls (and boys!) that STEM is for everyone.

There are so many unsung women in STEM whose stories deserve to be told. How do I decide which ones to write about?

Since I'm a computer scientist, who better to write about than Ada Byron Lovelace, the world's first computer programmer? Notice, I didn't say the first *woman* programmer. Ada was the first person, male or female, to write code for a computer.

At the time I started doing research for the book (about 2007 or so), no one, other than a few other computer geeks like me, had ever heard of Ada's accomplishments. I'm happy that my book *Ada Byron Lovelace and the Thinking Machine* has played a part in changing that.

You can tell by the title of my next book, *Grace Hopper: Queen of Computer Code*, that I still had more to say about women and computers. Grace was the first person (again, not just the first woman) to use words—instead of just 1s and 0s—to write computer code. This made it possible for nontechnical people (like kids!) to program computers.

For my third book, *Hedy Lamarr's Double Life: Hollywood Legend and Brilliant Inventor*, I decided it was time to consider women other than computer scientists. Hedy was a glamorous movie star AND she coinvented the technology that helps keep Wi-Fi, GPS, and Bluetooth from being hacked. I was drawn to Hedy's story because it shows kids they don't have to give up their other interests to be good at STEM.

I love bringing to life stories about women in STEM. Will I ever write biographies of men or people not in STEM? Who knows? But I do know that my books will always be about someone whose accomplishments have been overlooked—someone whose story deserves to be told.

 Ray Anthony Shepard

Ray Anthony Shepard is an octogenarian who writes biographies for his grandchildren and their generation. He grew up in Lincoln, Nebraska, a city reluctantly named for the slain president, and now lives in Lincoln, Massachusetts, a few miles from the Lexington-Concord battleground and the Paul Revere capture site. For more information, visit www.rayanthonyshepard.com.

Nonfiction Mentor Texts

Grades 4–8; 5–8; 7–8; PB, LF; Bio/SS

Shepard, Ray Anthony. *A Long Time Coming: The Ona to Obama Chronicles.* New York: Boyds Mills/Calkins Creek, 2022. (Grades 7–8)

_____. *Now or Never! 54th Massachusetts Infantry's War to End Slavery.* Honesdale, PA: Boyds Mills/Calkins Creek, 2017. (Grades 5–8)

_____. *Runaway: The Daring Escape of Ona Judge.* New York: Farrar, Straus and Giroux, 2021. (Grades 4–8)

Old Stories Made New

It's mid-twentieth century in the Midwest. I'm in an experimental program for poor kids at the University of Nebraska Laboratory School, and I'm sinking lower at my fifth-grade desk.

What's forcing me to take cover, as if practicing our monthly atomic bomb drill, is not the Russians but the morning lesson—slavery! All eyes have turned to me. Instead of being a friend and classmate, I'm a ten-year-old antagonist in a four-hundred-year-old drama.

It's more than simply being one of the few Black students in the school (or state); it's my family history. My grandfather was enslaved in Missouri until he was six years old. My mother filled me with stories of him and his father, who was also his master. Whiplashed between schoolbook lessons about slavery and home stories about defying slavery in ways small and large, I gradually learned enough to spin me toward teaching, educational publishing, and now nonfiction storytelling—an attempt to correct the damage done.

Fast-forward seventy years: the story's the same but in need of retelling.

Since my retirement, I have launched an encore career: writing biographies for young readers about the African American experience, real-life stories that give readers an affirmative perspective on the many ways people stood up to racial oppression and its flawed assumption of a human hierarchy. It's my attempt to do what I failed to do as a fifth grader, a middle school teacher, and a textbook editor.

Near my old office in Boston is the famous bronze by Augustus Saint-Gaudens, *The Shaw Memorial*, which I walked past twice a day every weekday. It's a moving tribute to the Union's first Black Civil War regiment. The beauty of the sculpture and the power of the purpose etched on the faces of the men stunned me when I first saw it. And over the years, I pledged that one day I would tell their story—the story of free Black soldiers and white officers who, in the words of Corporal James Henry Gooding, were willing to sacrifice themselves on the "altar of freedom" to liberate four million enslaved Americans.

Their story became my first book, *Now or Never! 54th Massachusetts Infantry's War to End Slavery*. It's a dual biography of two soldiers who served as war correspondents and whose regiment fought two wars: a two-year to-the-death fight against the Confederate Army and an eighteen-month battle with their own government for pay equality. Their story illustrates why 75 percent of the African American men of military age in the North risked being killed in battle or executed if captured to end American slavery. And because it's told through their war dispatches, it counters the myths that all African Americans were illiterate and that they played no part in the Union victory.

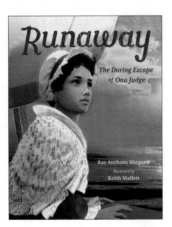

My second book, *Runaway: The Daring Escape of Ona Judge*, a picture book, tells the story of Ona Judge, her defiance of Martha and George Washington, and her decision to live a hardscrabble life as a fugitive rather than return to Mount Vernon as a pampered and privileged slave. Ona's independent spirit in choosing liberty over "comfortable" enslavement is the story I want my grandchildren and all other young readers to know.

My young adult collective biography, *A Long Time Coming: The Ona to Obama Chronicles*, helps readers understand the role of race in American history and how it continues to impact the United States today. Told in verse, it begins with the question:

> Have you ever wondered
> why we separate, perpetuate,
> and hyphenate Americans
> as if the hyphen means
> more-or-less-American?

I answer that question through the lives of Ona Judge, Frederick Douglass, Harriet Tubman, Ida B. Wells, Martin Luther King Jr., and Barack Obama—and their 250-year quest to transform the United States into the world's first multiracial democracy.

My goal is to tell old stories in a new and visceral way that helps young readers understand the past without shame, guilt, or resentment. I write not to be didactic but to be corrective, to show the universal desire for fairness. I strive to make readers, regardless of ethnicity, the *protagonists* rather than the victims or villains of racial ignorance and arrogance. My books highlight those who dedicated their lives to the basic human need for justice and liberty.

Sarah Albee

Sarah Albee is the *New York Times* bestselling author of more than one hundred books for young readers. She divides her time between living at the library and traveling around the country, visiting K–8 schools and talking with kids about history, writing, and books. Visit her at www.sarahalbeebooks.com.

Nonfiction Mentor Texts

Grades 5–8; LF; SS/STEM

Albee, Sarah. *Bugged: How Insects Changed History.* New York: Bloomsbury/Walker, 2014.

_____. *Poison: Deadly Deeds, Perilous Professions, and Murderous Medicines.* New York: Crown/Penguin Random House, 2017.

_____. *Poop Happened! A History of the World from the Bottom Up.* New York: Bloomsbury/Walker, 2010.

_____. *Why'd They Wear That: Fashion as the Mirror of History.* Washington, DC: National Geographic, 2015.

Let You Shine Through

At school visits, kids always ask me where I get my ideas. I talk about how it's important to keep a notebook handy. Ideas can show up suddenly, often when you're busy doing something besides sitting at your desk, and snagging them can require lightning-quick reflexes, like capturing the snitch in a Quidditch game.

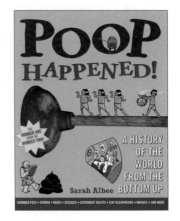

I usually tell them an amusing story about how I got the idea for my book *Poop Happened!* in a flash one day, just after my two-year-old son flushed his Super Balls down the toilet and stopped it up, an hour before fifteen people were due to show up at our house for a dinner party.

But honestly? That's an incomplete picture of how writers get their ideas. Ideas can percolate inside us for a long time. They can bubble up from our depths when we least expect them.

Because as every nonfiction writer knows, and as every teacher who reads a lot of student writing knows, the best writing stems from who the writer is and what they care most deeply about. Writing epiphanies are not random.

The fact is that questions about sanitation and other details about everyday life have interested me since I was a child. Yeah, I was THAT kid. I wanted to know how a knight in a suit of armor went to the bathroom. I wanted to know what kind of real-life poison might have been in Snow White's apple. I wanted to know why those kids in portraits I saw at the museum were wearing corsets and long skirts and crazy ruffled collars.

So here's *my* backstory.

My grandparents on my mother's side emigrated from Sicily to New York City in 1918. My mother, the oldest of five kids, grew up in a tenement on the

Lower East Side. Her family shared one toilet with three other families on her floor. She learned English, but my grandparents never did. My grandfather was a street sweeper, working for the department of sanitation.

When I was a kid, I begged my mother to tell me stories about her childhood—the shared toilet, the bedbugs, the shabby neighborhood. Those stories became part of who I am. (Also, it wasn't until about third grade that I realized other kids' grandparents knew how to speak English.)

As for my father—he was a professor, and in some ways, a rather eccentric man.

He wrote a lot about the power of preventive approaches to many public health issues. While other kids were sitting on their parent's knee listening to *Goodnight Moon*, I was hearing about how in 1854 John Snow deduced that cholera was waterborne and convinced public officials in London to remove the handle of the Broad Street pump.

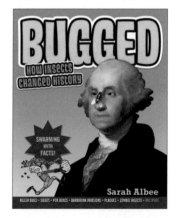

So the flash of inspiration I had the day of my dinner party was not random. Nor was my idea to write a book about epidemic diseases that happened at a time in the not-so-distant-past when insects were part of everyone's lives.

Or about history through fashion. That book idea evolved to become less about the one percenters who wore the fashionable clothes and more about the people who picked the cotton, dyed the fabric, and sewed the clothing.

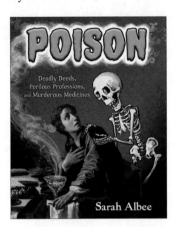

Or about the importance of regulations to prevent ordinary working people from being poisoned by radium, lead, arsenic, nicotine, and other toxins.

When I talk to new writers just starting out on the path to publication, I give them an exercise to do: Think about the authors out there that you admire. Now say their name, and quickly come up with a word or phrase that you associate with their writing. For instance:

Melissa Stewart: a celebration of science

Loree Griffin Burns: a love of nature

Jess Keating: zoology/funny animal facts

Then I tell them: Play this word association game about future-you. How do you want your future readers to describe you as a writer, five or seven or ten books from now? I suggest that they consider choosing topics that help amplify to the world the things *they* truly care about.

This exercise works with student writers, too.

The best writing, both nonfiction and fiction, reflects who we are as people and what we care about most deeply.

◎ Mary Kay Carson

Mary Kay Carson is the author of more than fifty nonfiction books for young people about nature, animals, space, inventors, weather, and history. She and her photographer husband, Tom Uhlman, are a veteran Scientists in the Field team, with six titles in the award-winning series. Mary Kay blogs with *STEM Tuesday* and *Hands-On-Books*. Visit her at www.Mary KayCarson.com.

Nonfiction Mentor Texts

Grades 5–8; LF; STEM

Carson, Mary Kay. *The Bat Scientists.* Boston: Houghton Mifflin Harcourt, 2010.

_____. *Emi and the Rhino Scientist.* Boston: Houghton Mifflin Harcourt, 2010.

_____. *Park Scientists: Gila Monsters, Geysers, and Grizzly Bears in America's Own Backyard.* Boston: Houghton Mifflin Harcourt, 2014.

A Glimpse of Lives Not Lived

Why do I choose to write books about meteorologists, biologists, astronomers, and ecologists? Because it allows me—a failed scientist—to live vicariously.

Growing up, animals were all I cared about. My family moved a lot, so pets were often my best friends. By the end of third grade, I'd lived in five states and attended four elementary schools. But Ralph the rat, Catzan, Lady Vain and her kittens, terrier Trixie, and an assortment of other pets happily kept me company. I fed and played with them, always wondering what it was like to be a goldfish or gerbil. Was it better?

I read animal encyclopedias, wrote school papers titled "Rats: Friend or Foe?," and yearned to be adopted by wild animals like the lucky kids in *Incident at Hawk's Hill* and *Julie of the Wolves*. Humans didn't understand me; maybe a mother badger would.

When college time finally arrived, I bolted from home with plans to become the next Dian Fossey. I would live in the woods with my animal subjects, who would accept me as one of their own. Who needs people anyway? So judgy.

That didn't happen. Instead, I ended up a science writer and nonfiction children's book author. (A *desk* job? shudders my twenty-year-old self.) But writing about scientists provides a window into a life not lived for me. And isn't that what all literature is—a chance to be someone or something else? To know what it's like to be a soldier mouse, ancient king, or sentient tree? Unlike in fiction, in nonfiction it just happens that the characters are real people, the dialogue actual quotes, and the plot true events. The result is the same.

Emi, the Sumatran rhino mother in *Emi and the Rhino Scientist,* is just as big a character in the book as Terri Roth, the reproductive physiologist who helps Emi have the first calf of its kind in captivity in more than a century. There are fewer than one hundred Sumatran rhinos left on Earth, so part of the motivation for writing the book was to help educate the public and donate a bit of money. Failed scientists can still help animals!

The book's photographer, Tom Uhlman (my husband), and I have deep ties to the Cincinnati Zoo, where Terri Roth works. I went to a year of high school there, spending mornings cleaning aardvark cages and filling little crocks with cow's blood for the vampire bats. Tom was a teenage member of the Junior Zoologists club. The zoo's blood-slurping bats ended up on the cover of *The Bat Scientists*.

I often employ a you-are-there technique when writing Scientist in the Field series books. Why? It engages readers. But it's also because I was actually there in a Texas pecan grove all night long helping scientists net and band bats. We really did look for radio-tagged Gila monsters with a herpetologist in Saguaro National Park and got soaking wet camping in the Smokies with an evolutionary ecologist while researching *Park Scientists*. Being there is the best part for me; why not share that with readers?

And while I make a living as a writer, I'm still a nature lover who feels connected to animals and often exasperated by humans. Science has always helped me make sense of the world. I believe things happen for a reason, but one that usually involves natural selection, gravitational forces, and/or geologic time.

Understanding animals, stars, storms, ecosystems, and gluons more deeply connects us to the world. And everybody craves connection. It's the currency of what matters, what motivates. Nonfiction writers have profoundly personal connections to their chosen subjects. We've got skin in the game. Our writing reflects that—and ourselves.

Gail Jarrow

Gail Jarrow writes for ages ten and up about history, science, and the history of science. Her books have received numerous awards, distinctions, and starred reviews. Gail's Deadly Diseases trilogy includes *Red Madness*, *Fatal Fever*, and *Bubonic Panic*. *Blood and Germs* is part of her Medical Fiascoes trilogy. Other award-winning books are *Spooked!* and *The Poison Eaters*. Gail lives in Ithaca, New York. Visit her at https://gailjarrow.com.

Nonfiction Mentor Texts

Grades 5–8; LF; STEM/SS

Jarrow, Gail. *Bubonic Panic: When Plague Invaded America*. Honesdale, PA: Boyds Mills/ Calkins Creek, 2016.

_____. *Fatal Fever: Tracking Down Typhoid Mary*. Honesdale, PA: Boyds Mills/Calkins Creek, 2015.

_____. *Red Madness: How a Medical Mystery Changed What We Eat*. Honesdale, PA: Boyds Mills/Calkins Creek, 2014.

_____. *Spooked! How a Radio Broadcast and* The War of the Worlds *Sparked the 1938 Invasion of America*. Honesdale, PA: Boyds Mills/Calkins Creek, 2018.

The Yellow Chalk Circle

I'm a writer because I can't help it. I choose to write nonfiction because I'm inquisitive and (politely) nosy. I didn't recognize curiosity in myself until I saw the giant yellow chalk circle.

When I was in fourth grade, the school band director visited our class every week to give us recorder lessons. Most of us, including me, had never played a musical instrument before. A few weeks into our lessons, he drew a huge circle on the chalkboard in yellow chalk.

"This," he said, "represents all there is to know about music." Then he put a tiny yellow dot in the center of the circle. I could barely see it from my seat in the back row. "This," he said, pointing to the dot, "is how much you know about music right now."

My initial reaction was discouragement. "Oh," I thought, "there's SO much to learn." But my next thought was, "I can't wait." For the first time, I had a sense of the vastness of human knowledge. I realized how many different big chalk circles there were for me to fill in. Music, science, math, history—everything!

Soon after, my mother bought me a set of *The World Book Encyclopedia*. Whenever I asked a question, she'd send me to the encyclopedia to look up the answer. And I found it . . . without an adult's help. Through reading, I had the power to learn on my own. I have never given away the old encyclopedia set.

Even as a nine-year-old, I knew there was more to the bare facts in encyclopedias and textbooks. Living in a small town, I was aware of the backstories of my classmates because many of our parents and grandparents had grown up together. I saw that family situations, tragedies, and triumphs shaped people.

Now, as a writer, I believe that personal details pull young readers into nonfiction books. After all, what is history without the individuals who created it? As characters in a true story, they drive the action.

These people make scientific discoveries and save lives the way Dr. Joseph Goldberger did in *Red Madness*, my book about pellagra. Some of them stop epidemics the way public health officials did in *Bubonic Panic*. Others, like typhoid-carrier Mary Mallon in *Fatal Fever*, unwittingly force doctors and governments to change their approach to disease. I want my readers to meet these real-life characters up close.

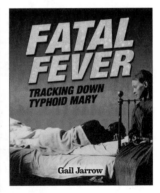

As a researcher, I'm (politely) nosy about other people's lives. To uncover the dynamic personalities behind the dry facts, I seek out the characters' own voices.

Autobiographies, interviews, and oral histories are useful. But the most valuable resources are diaries and letters, especially those the author never intended the world to see. There, in unguarded words, I find a more revealing picture.

When I worked on *Spooked! How a Radio Broadcast and* The War of the Worlds *Sparked the 1938 Invasion of America*, I read two thousand letters and telegrams written by radio listeners in the wake of the broadcast. Their emotional comments, expressing either outrage or delight or embarrassment, enabled me to show how ordinary Americans responded to the terrifying program on Halloween Eve 1938.

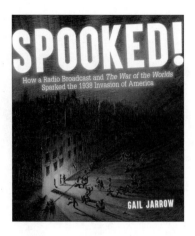

My curiosity leads me to topics about which I often know very little. But by the time I complete my research and begin to write, a tiny dot has expanded to fill yet another chalk circle.

I hope my work helps young readers experience the same excitement and satisfaction I felt playing my first musical instrument and tracking down an answer in the *World Book*. I always include a More to Explore section in my back matter so that the inquisitive ones can fill in their own chalk circles.

⊚ Anita Silvey

Former editor-in-chief of *Horn Book Magazine* and publisher of children's books at Houghton Mifflin, Anita Silvey has written several reference books about children's books—*Children's Books and Their Creators, 100 Best Books for Children,* and *Everything I Need to Know I Learned from a Children's Book.* Her nonfiction books for young readers have won numerous awards and citations, including the Sugarman Award.

Nonfiction Mentor Texts

Grades 5–8; LF; Bio/STEM, Bio/SS

Silvey. Anita. *I'll Pass for Your Comrade: Women Soldiers in the Civil War.* New York: Clarion, 2008.

_____. *Let Your Voice Be Heard: The Life and Times of Pete Seeger.* New York: Clarion, 2016.

_____. *The Plant Hunters: True Stories of Their Daring Adventures to the Far Corners of the Earth.* New York: Farrar, Straus and Giroux, 2012.

_____. *Undaunted: The Wild Life of Biruté Mary Galdikas and Her Fearless Quest to Save Orangutans.* Washington, DC: National Geographic, 2019.

_____. *Unforgotten: The Wild Life of Dian Fossey and Her Relentless Quest to Save Mountain Gorillas.* Washington, DC: National Geographic, 2021.

_____. *Untamed: The Wild Life of Jane Goodall.* Washington, DC: National Geographic, 2015.

Choosing Subjects for Nonfiction

Like all nonfiction writers, I get hundreds of recommendations from people about books they'd like me to create. Recently, even one of my savvy publishing friends suggested that I tackle the life of Roger Williams of Rhode Island, an unlikely idea for me since he represents the patriarchy.

I can write only about the subjects that personally resonate with me, that allow me to explore issues of concern. One example is my trilogy of books about three remarkable women scientists, Louis Leakey's protégés sometimes called "The Ape Ladies"—*Untamed: The Wild Life of Jane Goodall, Undaunted: The Wild Life of Biruté Mary Galdikas and Her Fearless Quest to Save Orangutans,* and

Unforgotten: The Wild Life of Dian Fossey and Her Relentless Quest to Save Mountain Gorillas.

All three subjects met my test for an ideal topic for a book:

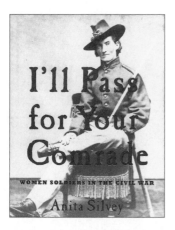

- I admire all three women and could give two to five years of my life researching and writing about them.
- The resulting books added to categories of nonfiction that we need—women scientists and the environment.
- I could do interesting primary research.
- I could add to existing information by interviews with key people.
- All were "true believers," people who gave everything for their cause.

My reasons for choosing these subjects reveal a great deal about my own concerns, my own issues. I realized ten years into my career as a nonfiction author that I had written about the same kind of person, again and again. All can be described as true believers. They have no cynicism; they hold nothing back; they give everything they have to their work and their cause.

Whether they are the women who dressed up as men to fight in the Civil War (*I'll Pass for Your Comrade*), or the plant hunters who traveled the earth to serve botanical science (*The Plant Hunters*), or Pete Seeger, who never stopped protesting (*Let Your Voice Be Heard*), all of them sacrificed everything, sometimes even their lives, for what they believed in and held dear.

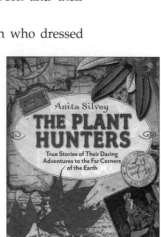

Now, I prefer staying at the Ritz rather than camping out, and my idea of a good time is snuggling up with a book, not traveling the world or running out onto a battlefield. But with my subjects I share one important trait that has framed my life: I am also a true believer.

I believe in the power and importance of children's books; I've championed children's books, fiction and nonfiction, for more than fifty years, from my first story hours for children to the present day.

In talking to hundreds of people to compile *Everything I Need to Know I Learned from a Children's Book,* I found that one-quarter of them chose careers based on childhood reading. Many fell in love with a person or character who became a role model, and many identified social and political causes they later embraced.

All reading is important. Childhood reading lasts an entire lifetime. I write nonfiction for children to inspire young readers, hoping that one of my books may help them realize that they, too, can devote their lives to an important cause. Like the subjects of my books, I am a true believer who wants to encourage the same trait in the next generation.

⊚ Steve Sheinkin

Steve Sheinkin's nonfiction titles include *The Notorious Benedict Arnold*, *Bomb*, *The Port Chicago 50*, *Most Dangerous*, *Undefeated* and *Born to Fly*. His books have received a Newbery Honor, three National Book Award finalist honors, three Boston Globe–Horn Book Awards for nonfiction, and a Sibert Medal. Visit Steve online at http://stevesheinkin.com.

Nonfiction Mentor Text
Grades 6–8; LF; Bio/SS

Sheinkin, Steve. *The Notorious Benedict Arnold: A True Story of Adventure, Heroism & Treachery*. New York: Flashpoint, 2010.

Finding My "Real" Writing

In my late twenties, I got a job writing history textbooks. I figured I'd keep it only until my "real" writing—short stories and screenplays—started to take off.

Ten years later, I was still writing textbooks.

It was a good news-bad news kind of thing. On the one hand, I was being paid to research and write. This was my 10,000 hours (and more) of practice, and I learned a lot about how to be efficient and precise with language. On the other hand, I was well aware that we were producing boring books. I kept finding stories I thought would make history more appealing and memorable to young readers, and the editors kept cutting them out. Anything funny, gross, shocking, controversial—all disallowed.

Take Benedict Arnold. I always tried to get in some Arnold action, with no luck. "Just mention the traitor part," was the editors' usual reply. It was frustrating. We're trying to convince kids that history can be exciting, and we waste this epic tale of action and adventure, spying and romance (Arnold should definitely have his own musical). Part of the problem was just a lack of room for stories, but I sensed there was more to the editors' attitude, and when I pushed for an explanation, a very experienced editor explained:

"Benedict Arnold makes people nervous."

How so? Well, Arnold was a hero first, then a villain. A good guy *and* a bad guy. We were writing books for upper elementary and middle school, and the worry was that this moral ambiguity would be confusing to kids. And get our books in trouble with adults.

But the thing is, American history is full of moral ambiguity. We're a nation founded on beautiful ideals written down by people who bought and sold other human beings—just to take the most obvious example. If talking about our history doesn't make us nervous, we're not doing it right.

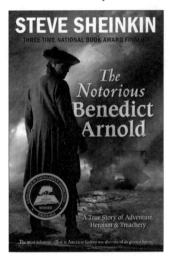

Only after this experience did I begin to see what my "real" writing should be. I'd take the true stories I'd been stuffing into files for years and tell them in a fast-paced, cinematic way. And I'd include the nervous-making parts.

So it's no coincidence that the rise and fall of Benedict Arnold was the subject of my first attempt at narrative nonfiction. I was so excited to start that I suggested to my wife, "Let's take all our vacation at once this year and go on a Benedict Arnold road trip!"

She agreed. She's a history nerd, and proud of it.

Starting in Arnold's hometown of Norwich, Connecticut (he still makes them nervous), we drove, hiked, and paddled all over the Northeast and into Quebec, stopping in all the places he lived, loved, fought, and drove his fellow Americans crazy. I collected stories and made sketches and took hundreds of photos.

And then we got back home, and I realized I had no idea how to write the kind of book I had in mind.

It took a while. But I kept going because I sensed this was the right story for the writer I was trying to become. And from there, with slightly more confidence, I dove into topics like the making of the atomic bomb and a Civil Rights story from World War II, and by then, to my surprise, this had become my job. It's not one I ever meant to have, but I wouldn't trade it now for anything.

In the Classroom

Whether you've read all the essays in this chapter or just a few, it's easy to see a commonality among them. Nonfiction authors choose topics that resonate deeply with them, often for reasons only they can understand. The ideas may trace back to childhood curiosity, a deeply held belief, or even a missed opportunity.

At the beginning of this chapter, I mentioned that I write about science because I'm fascinated by the natural world. I'm constantly encountering things that make me ask questions, and to satisfy my curiosity, I want to know more, more, more. But why? Why do I approach the world in this way? The answer lies in a powerful childhood memory.

When I was growing up, my parents owned ten acres of land on one side of the road. Across the street was a national forest. On weekends, my father, brother, and I often explored the woods around us. As we hiked, my dad frequently asked us questions:

"Why do stone walls run through the middle of the woods?"

"Why do sassafras trees have three different kinds of leaves?"

"Why don't chipmunks build their nests in trees like squirrels?"

He wanted us to think about our surroundings, and he knew a guessing game would be more engaging than a lecture.

One day, as we reached the top of a hill, my dad stopped and scanned the landscape. Then he asked if we noticed anything unusual about that area of the woods.

My brother and I looked around. We looked at each other. We shook our heads. But then, suddenly, the answer came to me. "All the trees seem kinda small," I said.

My dad nodded his approval. He explained that there had been a fire in the area about twenty-five years earlier. All the trees had burned and many animals had died, but over time the forest had recovered.

It was an aha moment. I instantly understood the power of nature. I also realized that a field, a forest, any natural place has stories to tell, and I could discover those stories just by paying attention.

I was hooked. Ever since, I've wanted to learn as much as I can about the natural world and share it with other people. Writing gives me the opportunity to do that.

If your students need support developing a spirit of inquiry, you can use or adapt some of the activities that enrichment specialist Jeanne Muzi suggests in her January 2017 *ASCD Education Update* article, "Road Tested / Five Ways to Strengthen Student Questioning." You can also encourage students to record questions on sticky notes and add them to a Wonder Wall bulletin board in your classroom. When students find an answer to one of the questions, they can write it on another sticky note and place it next to the question. They may also want to add the idea to the classroom Idea Board.

Even though students in grades 4–8 may not have enough life experience to understand their unique passions and perspectives the way adult writers do, they can still learn strategies for choosing topics that are related to their personal interests (information they find fascinating, questions inspired by their curiosity) and ideas that matter to them.

Strategy 1: Idea Board

To help intermediate students keep track of potential topics, you could create an Idea Board in your classroom. It shouldn't be hard to convince them to start making contributions, especially if you show them my Idea Board (see page 11) and share excerpts from some of the mentor authors' essays.

- Lita Judge, Don Tate, Michelle Markel, and Miranda Paul reveal connections between their personal interests and what they write about.
- Patricia Valdez, Susan Hood, Lesa Cline-Ransome, and Mara Rockliff explain why they write about ideas that matter to them.
- Teresa Robeson and Laurie Wallmark discuss how their writing combines personal interests with ideas that matter to them.

If students seem to struggle with this activity, try brainstorming some ideas with your class and add them to the Idea Board as models.

Students should continue adding ideas to the classroom Idea Board whenever they think of them. Remind your class that ideas are around them all the time.

Strategy 2: Idea Incubator

Because most middle school students move from classroom to classroom, an Idea Board may not work well at these grade levels. But students at any grade level can keep a bulleted list of potential topics on the last page of their writer's notebook. Every time they have an idea or question about something they see, read, or experience, they can add it to their Idea Incubator list. They can also include cool facts they come across.

If you teach grade 4 or 5, you can draw on the mentor essay examples mentioned above. If you teach in a middle school, you can use examples from the authors who write books intended for them:

Idea Incubator
- Fruits and vegetables used to look much different. They were smaller or had less "meat." They were bred like dogs and cats.
- Do insect eggs have a yolk like chicken eggs?
- The earliest tyrannosaurs were the same size as people.
- Some pirates were girls. Mary Read
- There are about 20 cocoa beans in a pod. That's how many are in a chocolate bar. What size bar?

• Sarah Albee and Mary Kay Carson describe how lifelong interests lead to the topics they select, while Gail Jarrow's curiosity inspires her to explore people and topics she doesn't know much about.

• Steve Sheinkin's topic selection process is more goal oriented. He looks for fascinating true stories from the past that can be presented in a fast-paced, cinematic way.

• Ray Anthony Shepard looks for real-life stories that show ways people stood up to racial oppression, while Anita Silvey searches for subjects who were "true believers"—people who dedicated their lives to a specific purpose or cause.

When it's time to start a nonfiction writing project, students can use their Idea Incubator list to develop an idea. If students are choosing their own topic, they may be able to pull an idea directly from their list. But even if you assign an umbrella topic that aligns with your content area curriculum, a list of facts, ideas, and questions is still a valuable tool. Working alone or with a partner, students can search for a common thread among the items on their list and brainstorm ways to apply that to the umbrella topic.

For example, let's say your class is studying the American Revolutionary War, and you want everyone to write a report related to that umbrella topic. Obvious choices might be George Washington or the Battle of Bunker Hill. But as a student looks at her Idea Incubator list, she notices a lot of facts, questions, and ideas about the weather and wonders if she could write a report about the weather during the Revolutionary War. After doing some research, she discovers that the 1770s were an exceptionally cold, snowy period in history, and the weather influenced the outcome of many battles. Bingo! She's identified a great topic that she's excited about.

Another student notices that his list includes some facts, questions, and ideas about numbers and math. He might decide to create a series of infographics

If making a list is a challenge for some students, or if they forget to do it, you could also try an Idea Jar. Think about your students. Some are probably idea-generating machines. They can help struggling classmates by focusing on the one idea that speaks to them most and adding their other ideas to the classroom Idea Jar.

You can add ideas, too. It's a way to anonymously provide guidance rather than dictate a topic. And because you aren't usurping your students' power to choose, they'll be able to take ownership of the project and the process.

comparing statistics related to different battles or the two competing armies. A third student who's fascinated by fashion could focus on the kind of clothing the soldiers wore, including how a severe shortage of boots affected the Colonial troops.

When a student's personal interests guide the research and writing processes, their final piece is bound to burst with passion and personality. An Idea Incubator list can help students recognize their natural interests and look for ways to discuss an umbrella topic through that lens.

Strategy 3: One Amazing Thing

Author Jess Keating (whose essay is included in Chapter 2) recommends an idea-generating technique that she calls "One Amazing Thing" (Keating, 2018). Each morning, students draw an empty box in their writer's notebook, write the words *One Amazing Thing* above it, and then close their notebook. Throughout the day, they should be on the lookout for one thing that catches their attention or sparks their curiosity. It could be an object, an action, a snippet of conversation—anything at all.

The act of making space for an amazing thing will raise your students' awareness of the world around them. All day long their subconscious brain will be looking for a way to fill that little box.

After doing this activity for a few weeks, students may see some trends among the things they notice. Identifying these commonalities can help students discover what matters to them, which can assist them in choosing topics they're excited to explore and write about.

Choosing a topic is an important first step in the nonfiction writing process, but for student writing to shine, it's equally important for students to find a focus they're excited about. Chapter 2 provides suggestions for helping students narrow their topic and identify a unique approach.

Finding a Focus

Getting Started

For many years, creating "all-about books" has been the go-to informational writing project for students, especially in elementary classrooms. But it's time to rethink this assignment.

When students write an all-about book, their goal—their author purpose—is to provide a general overview of a topic, such as kangaroos or volcanoes or Egyptian mummies. This is the same goal professional children's book authors have when they write traditional nonfiction books for large series. These survey books, which are meant to offer young readers an age-appropriate introduction to a topic, feature a standard design and language that's clear, concise, and straightforward (Hepler, 1998; Kiefer, 2010).

Traditional nonfiction books are an important part of any well-rounded children's nonfiction collection. Because they contain a wealth of information, they're a good entry point for curious kids who want to explore a new topic. They're also perfect for the early stages of the research process when students are trying to gain a general understanding of a subject. But these books don't make good mentor texts for writing workshop. This has nothing to do with how talented the writer is and everything to do with the inherent differences between writing a broad overview of a topic versus taking a more focused approach. Simply put, writing in a generalized way limits a nonfiction writer's ability to craft rich, engaging text (Portalupi & Fletcher, 2001).

But when writers choose a topic they're passionate about and take an in-depth look at a specific idea, concept, theme, or question, they can be more playful and innovative. They can take advantage of a wide range of nonfiction craft moves to create prose that reflects their zeal for the subject (Dorfman & Cappelli, 2009; Kiefer, 2010).

For example, when nonfiction writers find a focus that excites them, they can select a format and text structure that complements their distinctive approach to the content (Clark, Jones, & Reutzel, 2013; Kerper, 1998; Williams

et al., 2007). They can also experiment with voice and language devices (Moss, 2003; Stewart & Young, 2018). Because writers of traditional nonfiction must cover a huge amount of information in a limited number of words, they don't have the same kind of opportunities to delight as well as inform.

Sometimes finding a focus for nonfiction writing is easy. For example, the idea for *A Seed Is the Start* came from a Pinterest board that showcased incredible close-up photos of seeds. I couldn't believe seeds came in so many different sizes and shapes, and that made me ask a question: How does a seed's external features contribute to its ability to survive and germinate?

After doing some research, I discovered that a seed's shape is closely related to how it disperses. Seeds can be transported by wind or water or by hitching a ride on an animal's fur. Some seeds even hop or creep across the ground.

I was fascinated, and I knew kids would be, too, so I decided to write a photo-illustrated book that celebrates the amazing ways seeds move from place to place.

Finding a focus for *Can an Aardvark Bark?* was an entirely different experience.

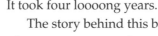

It took four loooong years.

The story behind this book began in March 2010 when my parents took our entire family on a trip to Disney World. At the time, my nephew was ten and my nieces were six and eight.

One day we decided to take a break from the rides and visit the Animal Kingdom, where we saw two adorable cotton-top tamarin monkeys. The informational plaque on their cage told us where the monkeys live, what they eat, and the sounds they make. It said they bark.

My nieces and nephew were skeptical. But then, as if on cue, the monkeys started vocalizing.

That night my nephew asked a great question: "Do you think there are a lot of different animals that bark?"

With the help of Google, we started making a list. By the end of our trip, we had identified more than twenty animals that bark.

When we got home, I started researching other animal sounds. After about six months, I had compiled a list of more than three hundred animals that bark, bellow, chirp, chatter, grunt, growl, and more. That's when I knew I had the makings of a book. But I still needed a focus. After all, I couldn't possibly share all the information I'd collected.

Should I focus on animals that bark and ignore all the other cool sounds I'd researched?

Should I write about the incredible diversity of sounds animals make to com-

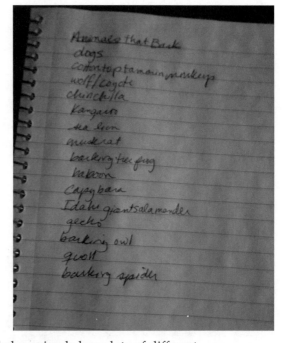

municate the same message? For example, baby animals have lots of different ways of getting their mothers' attention.

Or should I describe all the different messages that can be conveyed with a single sound?

In the end, I chose the third option—but not until I'd written a whole lot of rough drafts that didn't work. To find a focus, I had to experiment until I found just the right hook and text structure.

There are three things to take away from this discussion:

1.   Focused writing is inherently more engaging.

2.   Sometimes the focus is obvious from the start. Other times it takes a while for a writer to find the perfect lens for presenting information.

3.   Ideally, writers find their focus as part of the prewriting process. But it may not emerge until after writing a few (or many) drafts.

Essays by Mentor Authors

Now that you know a little bit about how I find a focus for the books I write, I encourage you to take a look at what some other authors have to say about this important part of their writing process. As I mentioned in Chapter 1, there's no single right way to write nonfiction. Hearing about a diverse array of experiences can help young writers develop a process that works for them.

If you have time, you may want to read all sixteen essays, but if not, Teacher Timesaver Table 2.1 will help you identify the ones that are of greatest value to you right now.

TEACHER TIMESAVER TABLE 2.1. A Guide to Mentor Essays about Finding a Focus

Author	Grade Level	Book Format*	Content Area*	Essay Highlights
Barbara Kerley	4–5	PB	Bio/SS, Bio/Arts, SS, STEM	To focus her topic, Barbara creates a sentence that helps her pinpoint a concept or theme she wants to explore.
Laura Purdie Salas	4–5	PB	STEM	Laura finds her focus by repeatedly asking, "What else?" to generate a list of related ideas.
Barb Rosenstock	4–6	PB	Bio/SS, Bio/Arts, Bio/STEM	Barb knows the focus of her biographies from the start. She begins with an idea, memory, or experience that has personal meaning to her and then chooses a person to profile.
Traci Sorell	4–6	PB	SS	Traci focuses on making the invisible visible.
Jess Keating	4–6	PB	STEM	Jess sees herself as a recruiter. She focuses her topics in ways that make readers pay attention, be astonished, and care about the world and all living creatures.
Jason Chin	4–6	PB	STEM	As Jason created *Grand Canyon*, he focused on conveying the "breathtaking" feeling he experienced as he viewed the canyon for the first time.
Chris Barton	4–8	PB	Bio/SS	When Chris was writing *What Do You Do with a Voice Like That?*, he focused on how Barbara Jordan recognized and chose to use her natural gift.
Carole Boston Weatherford	4–8	PB	Bio/SS	Carole focuses on sharing the African American freedom struggle with young readers to preserve history and honor famous and unsung heroes.
Sandra Neil Wallace	4–6, 5–8	PB, LF	Bio/SS	Sandra focuses on why and how some people move beyond fear to lead brave lives.
Anita Sanchez	4–6, 5–8	PB, LF	STEM	Anita focuses on getting kids out of the house and showing them that nature is a place that's safe, fun, and welcoming.
Tanya Lee Stone	4–6, 5–8	LF	Bio/SS, Bio/STEM, Bio/Arts	Tanya experiences a "moment of understanding" when she finally finds a focus for the true story she is trying to tell.
Kelly Milner Halls	5–8	LF	STEM	Kelly focuses on the idea that "weird is a wonder worthy of exploration."

Pamela S. Turner	5–8	LF	STEM	Because Pamela feels a deep connection to animals, she focuses on exploring our relationship with them and their relationships with one another.
Karen Romano Young	5–8	LF	STEM	Karen wants kids to know that science is for everyone. She focuses on helping her readers feel invited, included, involved, and validated.
Jennifer Swanson	5–8	LF	STEM	Because Jennifer has an insatiable curiosity, she focuses on seeking answers to her questions about the world.
Elizabeth Partridge	7–8	LF	Bio/SS, SS	Betsy's obsession with the Vietnam War led her to write about it three times, using different genres to shift her focus each time.

*Key to Abbreviations
Book Format: PB = picture book, LF = long form
Content Area: Bio = biography, SS = social studies/history, STEM = science/technology/engineering/math

After you've read the essays that seem best suited to your current needs, please turn to the In the Classroom section that begins on page 113. It provides a variety of practical ideas that can help you support students as they find a focus for the nonfiction pieces they write.

⊚ Barbara Kerley

Barbara Kerley is an award-winning author of nonfiction and fiction for kids. Her picture book biographies include *Eleanor Makes Her Mark, Tigers and Tea with Toppy, The Dinosaurs of Waterhouse Hawkins*, and *What to Do about Alice?* Her nonfiction concept books, illustrated with National Geographic photographs, include *Brave Like Me; One World, One Day*; and *The World Is Waiting for You*. She lives in Portland, Oregon. Visit her website at www.barbarakerley.com.

Nonfiction Mentor Texts

Grades 4–5; PB; Bio/SS, Bio/Arts, SS, STEM

Kerley, Barbara. *A Cool Drink of Water*. Washington, DC: National Geographic, 2002.

———. *The Extraordinary Mark Twain (According to Susy)*. New York: Scholastic Press, 2010.

———. *A Home for Mr. Emerson*. New York: Scholastic Press, 2014.

———. *A Little Peace*. Washington, DC: National Geographic, 2007.

———. *Those Rebels, John and Tom*. New York: Scholastic Press, 2012.

———. *With a Friend by Your Side*. Washington, DC: National Geographic, 2015.

Harriet and Me

Ever since I was a little kid, I've been super interested in other people. I like to think it's because I'm curious, but honestly, I think it's because I am this weird mix of really nosy and also pretty shy.

Starting in third grade and for years beyond, my favorite book—hands down—was *Harriet the Spy* by Louise Fitzhugh. The book's characters seemed so vivid and original. It really was unlike anything else I'd ever read, and I read it obsessively (so often, in fact, that I had to use stickers and duct tape on the book's spine to keep my copy from falling apart).

By the time I was a teen, I was an avid people watcher. I also got very involved in community and high school theater. And if you think about it, what else is theater but people-watching?

I'm fascinated by people's experiences, the choices they make, what their passions are, and how they choose to pursue them.

It's not really surprising to me that I'd be drawn to writing biographies. Early in the research process, I try to figure out: What is important to this person? How does it shape their life? And, through learning about them, what can we learn about life's possibilities?

So, when I'm thinking about the focus of a book, I try not to think in general terms (e.g., This is a book about Ralph Waldo Emerson. This is a book about John Adams and Thomas Jefferson. This is a book about Susy Clemens). I try instead to create a sentence that will give a shape to the story arc, a sentence that reveals character and explores a theme in a specific way:

A Home for Mr. Emerson
Ralph Waldo Emerson spent his life building community, and in his hour of need, his friends and neighbors came to his aid.

Those Rebels, John and Tom
John Adams and Thomas Jefferson had different values, lifestyles, and personalities, but they came together to cooperate for the good of the country.

The Extraordinary Mark Twain (According to Susy)
Susy Clemens was determined to write a biography of her father that would set the record straight.

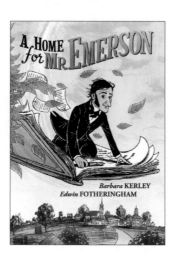  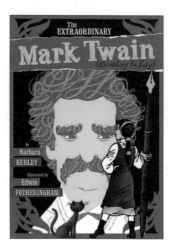

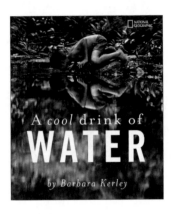
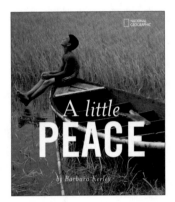
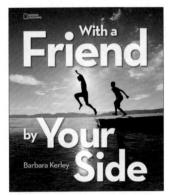

I see my fascination with people in full force in my expository writing as well. I write concept books with National Geographic, and each book explores a theme. My first book with National Geographic was *A Cool Drink of Water*, and it was inspired by my two years in the Peace Corps, from 1981 to 1983. I taught math, science, and English in a tiny town where the houses had thatched roofs, no electricity, and no running water.

And it was the fact that I had to walk with my jug down to the community water tap every day and carry my water home that led, many years later, to my book about water. I was back home in the United States, reading an issue of *National Geographic* magazine, when I turned the page and saw a photograph of two women in India carrying brass water pots on their heads. They looked so strong and yet so graceful. As soon as I saw the photo, I thought: I want to write about water, not just in Nepal but around the world. And happily, the photo that made me want to write the book is in the book.

Again, instead of thinking in general terms, I try to create a statement that gives the text a clear focus—what, specifically, do I want to say about this topic?

A Cool Drink of Water
In different ways around the world, we all drink water.

A Little Peace
Each of us can do small things to make the world more peaceful.

With a Friend by Your Side
Reach out to others, for life is better with friends.

My books have covered a huge range of topics, but at the core, they really have all been about people. Endlessly fascinating—especially to me.

 Laura Purdie Salas

Laura Purdie Salas is a former eighth-grade English teacher, a former copy editor (who has nightmares about errors on menus and signs), and a former magazine editor. She will *never* be a former reader. Laura is the author of many poetry and nonfiction books, including *Water Can Be . . .* , *BookSpeak!*, and *Lion of the Sky*. You can meet Laura at her website, laurasalas.com, where you can also access her resources for educators.

Nonfiction Mentor Texts

Grades 4–5; PB; STEM

Salas, Laura Purdie. *A Leaf Can Be . . .* Minneapolis, MN: Millbrook, 2012.

———. *Meet My Family! Animal Babies and Their Families.* Minneapolis, MN: Millbrook, 2018.

———. *A Rock Can Be . . .* Minneapolis, MN: Millbrook, 2015.

———. *Snowman – Cold = Puddle: Spring Equations*. Watertown, MA: Charlesbridge, 2019.

———. *Water Can Be . . .* Minneapolis, MN: Millbrook, 2014.

I Am Not a Robot

I try not to take it personally, but there's a common, crushing misconception that fiction is creative writing drawn from the depths of a writer's soul, while nonfiction is simply a recitation of facts that any basic robot could spit out.

The reality is very different. My personality, my beliefs, and my experiences are deeply embedded in the books I write.

My tendency to get bored easily, for example, didn't just lead to a revolving door of college majors. It also makes me gravitate toward poetry and picture books. They are intense, up-close, but brief examinations of a topic.

As I begin the writing process, I usually think about topics broadly and ask, "What else?" For example, *A Leaf Can Be . . .* began when I read an old poem I had written about Honduran tent bats and their leafy shelters. Some writers might have wanted to delve into that relationship in great detail. But because I like lists

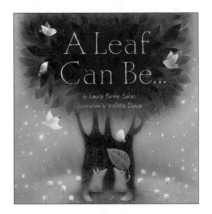

and variety, my question was not "Why?" or "How did they evolve to do that?" It was "What else do leaves do?" My brain is always thinking, "Show me something new."

Another way I am present in my Can Be . . . books, which include *Water Can Be* . . . and *A Rock Can Be* . . . , is that I have a deeply felt sense of justice, and I tend to root for the underdog. I find that exploring the wonders of underappreciated things is a common thread in my work.

My geographical history also influences my writing. Though I was born and raised in Florida, the rest of my family was Indiana-born. While growing up, I longed for real seasons that transformed my daily life, but Florida didn't offer that. My adopted state of Minnesota, how-ever, loves to show off its seasons! I find myself writing about seasons again and again, drawn to celebrating their beauty and unlocking their mysteries. I prob-ably wouldn't have done this if I had stayed in Florida.

With *Snowman – Cold = Puddle: Spring Equations*, the equations format came first—even before the topic. In my ideas journal, I wrote:

___ + ___ = _____ . Bees + flowers = honey. Short equation. Then longer prose explanation. All science related.

I wondered, "What else could I reveal through equations?" It turned out the hook was transformation. Anything that *changed* was ripe for some math magic. And spring is certainly a season of change in most areas. When the title equa-tion popped into my head, I loved it. And then I focused on what else changes in spring—in weather, in animals, in plants, etc.

Here's a sample: **bushes × blooms = perfume**

Lilac blooms are spring's perfume. The sweet scent invites insects and birds to visit. These important visitors track pollen from flower to flower, like tracking mud from room to room. Humans just enjoy the wonderful smells.

Another aspect of my life experiences that inspires and shapes my work is family history. When I was a kid, my family did not fit in. My parents had very strict ideas: five hours of TV per week; kids paid part of the electric bill; working harder in school even if you already had straight As; and mostly ignoring extended family.

I also have a sister with OCD, who washed her hands hundreds of times daily. Back then, that was just considered weird, not a medical condition. I had a mountain of family shame.

As a grown-up, I thought about species in which the siblings do a lot of the parenting, like meerkats. That reminded me of my big sisters and reassured me. So I asked, "What else?" (Show me something new.) What other species have social structures that have human parallels? *Meet My Family!* showcases different structures of animal families. But more importantly, it says to kids today who are embarrassed like I was, "Your family is okay. As long as you are loved, you are okay. You are okay." I don't think there's anything more important that I have to say to young readers.

So all my little quirks, loves, and fears shape the books that I write. I'd love to see more recognition that this is true for most nonfiction authors. And imagine all the exciting nonfiction that students will create as we encourage them to infuse *all* their writing—not just their fiction—with the qualities that make them who they are.

⊚ Barb Rosenstock

Barb Rosenstock loves true stories best. She writes historical picture books, including the Caldecott Honor title *The Noisy Paint Box*, illustrated by Mary Grandpré. Her work has been awarded an Orbis Pictus Honor, a Sydney Taylor Honor, and the Golden Kite, among others. Nonfiction titles include *Otis and Will Discover the Deep*, *Fight of the Century*, *The Secret Kingdom*, *Thomas Jefferson Builds a Library*, *Leave It to Abigail*, *Prairie Boy*, and more. Barb lives with her family near Chicago.

Nonfiction Mentor Texts

Grades 4–6; PB; Bio/SS, Bio/Arts, Bio/STEM

Rosenstock, Barb. *Otis and Will Discover the Deep: The Record-Setting Dive of the Bathysphere*. New York: Little, Brown, 2018.

———. *Prairie Boy: Frank Lloyd Wright Turns the Heartland into a Home*. Honesdale PA: Boyds Mills/Calkins Creek, 2019.

———. *Thomas Jefferson Builds a Library*. Honesdale, PA: Boyds Mills/Calkins Creek, 2013.

———. *Through the Window: Views of Marc Chagall's Life and Art*. New York: Knopf, 2018.

Connecting through Biography

The question I get asked most at school visits is "Why do you write biography?" Early on, that question caught me off-guard—the "why" of it never occurred to me.

To know why I write biography, you'd have to have met my grandpa, Stan. He was the kind of Chicago character who spent his life connecting people to jobs, tickets, schools, charities, and each other. He understood where people came from, and where they wanted to go. He knew how to keep a confidence and when to reveal. He connected people through stories—hilarious, tragic, or tender. He told people's stories better than anyone I have ever met.

I loved listening to his stories, and I was a voracious reader as a kid, but "author" was a job for fancy people in New York or Paris. As an adult, I worked in corporate marketing, had a family, and read a good deal to my sons. They too tended to like stories about people—explorers, inventors, and athletes. Although there has always been great children's nonfiction, many of the biographies I read to my sons (going back about fifteen years) disappointed me.

None of them sounded like my grandpa's stories. Few of them seemed connected to real kids' struggles or larger themes. They were essentially illustrated encyclopedia entries. So instead of reading the books as they were written, I used what I'd learned from my grandpa to

Barb with her grandpa.

turn the facts into stories my sons would love. At some point, I transitioned to writing.

When I visit schools, I find that many teachers and students make false assumptions about the process of writing biography. First off, they assume I have some "file of famous folks" in a desk drawer. They believe I go to the list, choose a person, do some research, and plug facts about the subject into some sort of formula. But biography isn't a formula (birth + 3 facts + death = fame). It's a way of *thinking* about art or science or sports or any topic through the lens of understanding who did what, why, and how.

Why do teachers and students have these misconceptions? Because that's often how students write reports in school. But that's not how professional writers work.

For me, the process of choosing a subject is complex and deeply rooted in who I am. In fact, I don't typically start with a person at all. I begin with an idea or a memory or an experience that has personal meaning to me. Here are the personal connections that launched a few of my titles:

Otis and Will Discover the Deep: As a child, I was fascinated by a TV cartoon called *Diver Dan*.

Prairie Boy: My father built our family home, and my early memories are of the sights, sounds, and smells of a home construction site.

Thomas Jefferson Builds a Library: In eighth grade, I wandered off into the library on a field trip to Monticello (Thomas Jefferson's home).

Through the Window: When I was a college student, Chagall's *America Windows* at the Art Institute of Chicago was my favorite place to meditate.

As you can see, my topic choices are influenced by what I want and *need* to write about. The biography subjects are just the way I present an idea I'm passionate about.

That's why no two biographies are the same. Even when two (or more) authors write about the same person, each one brings something different, something unique to the process. A finely crafted biography offers much more than a Wikipedia entry because, at its heart, is an idea the author has carried deep inside (sometimes for years). The author combines that idea with accurate research to craft a creative product that contains parts of the author's story within the subject's.

I write biography not because of who my subjects were, but because of who I am. I wish each child in every classroom the same opportunity to discover their own interests, backgrounds, and experiences—to use their own true stories to connect with others.

◎ Traci Sorell

Traci Sorell writes poems as well as fiction and nonfiction for young people. Before writing for children, Traci advocated for the rights of Native Nations and their citizens at the White House and US Congress. She is an enrolled Cherokee Nation citizen and lives in northeastern Oklahoma, where her tribe is located. For a complete list of her works, visit www.tracisorell.com.

Nonfiction Mentor Text

Grades 4–6; PB; SS

Sorell, Traci. *We Are Grateful: Otsaliheliga*. Watertown, MA: Charlesbridge, 2018.

Making the Invisible Visible for All

When I write nonfiction (or fiction, for that matter), I focus on making the invisible visible. If someone had asked about my focus five years ago when I began writing for children, I wouldn't have answered that way. Back then, I just wanted to have a picture book showing present-day Cherokee life and people to share with my young son, and none existed.

But my focus expanded when I realized how few contemporary books about Native life (nonfiction or fiction) there are when you consider there are more than 570 federally recognized tribes in the United States. Most books are written by people with no familiarity or knowledge of the tribe(s), people, land base, or history. This results in most of those books having inaccurate text and images that most readers take as fact.

I didn't realize the Cherokee or other Native Nations and their citizens were invisible until I was a teen. That's when my family moved from northeastern Oklahoma, where my tribe is located, to Southern California.

No one in my new community knew or understood that I was a dual citizen of the Cherokee Nation and the United States. Even the tribes from the San Diego area didn't figure into the local news or community events, and they certainly weren't included in the school curriculum. Talk about identity crisis.

This invisibility caused me to major in Native American Studies in college. I wanted to read, research, and know my own tribe's history and contributions. I wanted to learn more about other Native Nations, too.

After college, I pursued advanced degrees, studying how federal laws and policies impacted Native Nations and their inherent sovereignty. Not exactly what anyone in my family expected from a first-generation college graduate.

I find that a lot of abhorrent laws and policies get enacted and upheld in federal courts when stories are not told, when Indigenous people are invisible, and when the sovereignty of Native Nations is not honored. Devastating consequences result.

I want to shine a light on those injustices in my work so children know the history of what has happened—and continues to happen—in this country. Even if the history doesn't make it into textbooks, I want to see those stories available on school and public library shelves.

Native Nations and their citizens have made and continue to make so many amazing contributions, but those stories have rarely been told. When they have, it is usually in service to white-focused narratives, not the humanity, resiliency, and hard work of Indigenous peoples.

Knowing this, I plan to be busy the rest of my life actively recruiting other Native writers and artists to enter the world of children's literature. Our ability as Native Nations to remain sovereign, provide for our citizens, and contribute to the broader mainstream society depends on greater visibility and education of all children in the United States. Accurate books are critical to this effort.

I'm grateful for the Native creators who have already been doing the work in this field. I'm humbled to add my contributions to this effort.

My debut nonfiction picture book, *We Are Grateful: Otsaliheliga*, shares the value of gratitude as taught in contemporary Cherokee culture across the four seasons. My other nonfiction books focus on broader themes impacting all Native Nations as well as the contributions of individual tribal citizens. I want to do what I can to make sure Indigenous peoples are never overlooked, cast aside, or rendered invisible again.

⊚ Jess Keating

Jess Keating is an award-winning author, illustrator, and zoologist. She is the creator of more than a dozen children's books, including *Eat Your Rocks, Croc!*; *Bunbun & Bonbon*; *Shark Lady*; *Pink Is for Blobfish*; and the Elements of Genius middle grade series. To learn more about Jess, visit www.jesskeatingbooks.com, where she shares tips and tricks for creatives, book extras, and her weekly newsletter, *The Curious Creative*.

Nonfiction Mentor Texts

Grades 4–6; PB; STEM

Keating, Jess. *Cute as an Axolotl: Discovering the World's Most Adorable Animals*. New York: Knopf, 2018.

———. *Gross as a Snot Otter: Discovering the World's Most Disgusting Animals*. New York: Knopf, 2019.

———. *Pink Is for Blobfish: Discovering the World's Perfectly Pink Animals*. New York: Knopf, 2016.

———. *Shark Lady: The True Story of How Eugenie Clark Became the Ocean's Most Fearless Scientist*. Naperville, IL: Sourcebooks Jabberwocky, 2017.

———. *What Makes a Monster? Discovering the World's Scariest Creatures*. New York: Knopf, 2017.

A Life of Astonishment

I'm one of the lucky ones.

I know exactly why I'm here on this earth. That doesn't mean I've always known what I wanted to do as a career, mind you. But I knew what I loved. And to me, that's half the battle to finding your way.

I've always been a writer, but the decision to be an author—in particular, an author for children—happened in a flash.

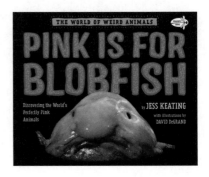

Trust a poet to provide the words I need here. Mary Oliver once said: "Pay attention. Be astonished. Tell about it."

I didn't realize it when I was younger, but those three steps form the key to why I'm here. I don't *try* to do these things, I *need to.* Paying attention, being astonished, and telling about it is my natural state.

Being a zoologist gave me the ability to pay attention and be astonished professionally. I was in graduate school when I realized the "tell about it" was missing. It was doing me no good to tell other scientists about what I was learning. I wanted to *tell the world.* I had things to say and needed to reach people who would get it. By *it*, I don't mean the facts.

I needed them to get the magic.

I woke up one day and said, "I'm going to write children's books."

Knowledge and wisdom are double-edged swords. The more you learn, the more you fall in love with the world, but the greater you feel the threat behind precious things.

We learn about fictional villains through books, but there are villains in real life, too. Do you want to know which villain scares me the most? The kid in *The Giving Tree* by Shel Silverstein. That kid terrifies me, because he exists in all of us if we let him. He's a taker. And he misses the point of *everything*.

Before I became an author, one of my jobs was at a wildlife rehabilitation center. We often received calls of wildlife in urban spaces, and one day I got a call from a McDonald's, telling me that a dead bird was "messing up their drive-thru" line. I prepared my things and made the short drive there.

It was a ring-necked gull. People often call them seagulls, but that's not really true. This bird was splayed by the drive-thru lane, its legs and wings at impossible angles. Hit by a car.

I steeled myself to clean him up. But as I knelt down to tuck his wing against his body, his eyes flashed open. Beautiful, bright-as-a-lemon eyes that cut right through me. Terrified. Hopeful.

He was *alive*. People were ordering their Big Macs a few feet away, and this creature was still alive, twisted and broken in terrible pain. He was surrounded but unseen. This moment has never left me.

I gave him medication for pain and moved him over to the side of the parking lot, where a cluster of trees was rustling above us in that early autumn way. I wanted him to see those leaves. When you work with animals enough, you get a sense when there's nothing more you can do.

But, I realized, there was *one* thing I could do. I didn't want him to die alone, in a greasy, littered fast-food drive-thru.

I couldn't save him, but I could *witness* him.

Maybe it sounds silly. I'm sure the people picking up their orders thought I was odd. But it didn't matter.

I don't know what kind of life he'd had, but I could make sure that *one* person on the planet was there to truly see him. I refused to let him remain unseen a moment longer. I stayed beside him until he was gone. I still hope that somewhere in there, he knew he mattered.

Every animal I've met has left an impact on me. To me, they've never been "animals." They feel like family. Some are what you might call majestic creatures. The wild wolf that stared me down on a hike in the woods. The pod of orcas that jumped joyously in the Arctic Ocean. Bears and sharks and eagles.

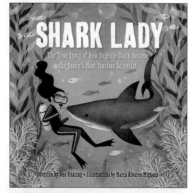

But some are like the ring-necked gull. Small. Unassuming. With a secret soul and message if you're just willing to witness it.

They all matter.

The truth is, I don't consider myself a nonfiction author at all. I'm not a writer. I'm a *recruiter*. My goal is to recruit readers and kids to the side of caring. To the side of empathy for those who aren't like themselves. Because that's the only way to ensure this world is protected from the real villains.

I write to pay attention and to astonish my readers. And maybe one day they'll tell about it, too.

Jason Chin

Jason Chin is an author and illustrator whose books include *Grand Canyon*, *Redwoods*, *Island*, and *Gravity*. He has received a Caldecott Honor, Sibert Honor, Orbis Pictus Award, Boston Globe–Horn Book Honor, and Gryphon Award. He lives in Vermont with his wife, Deirdre Gill, and their children. Visit Jason online at https://jasonchin.net.

Nonfiction Mentor Texts

Grades 4–6; PB; STEM

Chin, Jason. *Grand Canyon*. New York: Roaring Brook, 2017.

———. *Redwoods*. New York: Roaring Brook/Square Fish, 2009.

The Art of Crafting Nonfiction

When I was in high school, I rarely connected with the assigned reading, so I avoided it. With less practice, reading became more challenging, and during my years at art school, I stopped reading almost entirely.

When my mentor, Caldecott Medalist Trina Schart Hyman, found out, she was not happy. "Don't you know that artists have to read!" she exclaimed. And so I started reading again.

Eventually I picked up *A Short History of Nearly Everything* by Bill Bryson. It was entertaining, and I learned quite a bit of science, which made it particularly satisfying. After that, I found myself seeking out more and more books and articles about science.

In 2006, I read an article about redwood trees while riding the New York City subway, and it captured my imagination. I was transported to the redwood forest in my mind's eye. I imagined climbing the trees and swinging through the canopy with the scientists "like Spider-man in slow motion," as the author Richard Preston put it. That experience inspired me to write and illustrate *Redwoods*, and its success led to a career as a nonfiction author-illustrator for children.

For me, reading provides the raw materials for creativity. Novel ideas are rarely (if ever) generated from thin air. They come from combining ideas, memories, images, feelings, and experiences that already exist in my mind. For example, presenting to urban students who had never walked in a forest prompted me to make the main character of *Redwoods* a New York City school kid. And my memories of looking for Goldbug in Richard Scarry's books prompted me to add a flying squirrel to *Redwoods*.

When I conduct research, I am first and foremost seeking knowledge. I want to attain a level of expertise that will allow me to write from a position of authority. I want to know what the facts are, to understand the concepts, and to know why scientists believe them. Books are my primary resources, but I also watch movies, speak to experts, look at art, and seek direct experiences with the topic at hand. If I'm writing about a place, this means visiting that place.

As part of the research process for *Grand Canyon*, I booked a trip to Arizona to observe the canyon for myself. I wanted to learn what it looked like and to know what it felt like to be there. When I experienced the canyon's incredible vastness firsthand, I realized that describing its size in pictures would be an impossible challenge. You really do have to see it to believe it.

The first time I walked up to the edge of the canyon, I caught my breath and learned what the phrase "breathtaking" really means. I decided that I would try to create a book that brought this moment of surprise to readers. To do this, I purposely obscured the vastness of the canyon until the very end of the book, where I include a double gatefold panorama. I hope that when kids open the gatefold and are confronted with a painting twice the size of everything else they've seen, it will take their breath away, and they'll make an emotional connection to the canyon.

I like to think of science and art as two sides of the same coin. Both scientists and artists are seeking truth. Scientists seek objective truth by observing the world and removing themselves from the equation, while artists seek to express truths about their own experiences in the world. Science is objective, art is subjective, and we need them both.

I write about science because I want to know how the world works, and I want to share this knowledge with children. But to remember what they read, kids need a way to connect with the ideas and information. This is where art comes in.

As an artist, I'm concerned with story, character, and feeling, and I try to use these elements to connect with readers and activate their imaginations. I want my books to describe scientific concepts *and* elicit an emotional response from readers. To achieve this, I draw on the connections I forged with the subject during the research process.

@ Chris Barton

Chris Barton is the author of numerous picture books, including both fiction (*Shark vs. Train, Fire Truck vs. Dragon, Mighty Truck*) and nonfiction (*The Day-Glo Brothers: The True Story of Bob and Joe Switzer's Bright Ideas and Brand-New Colors, Whoosh! Lonnie Johnson's Super-Soaking Stream of Inventions, Dazzle Ships: World War I and the Art of Confusion, All of a Sudden and Forever: Help and Healing After the Oklahoma City Bombing*). He lives in Austin, Texas. Please visit him at www.chris barton.info.

Nonfiction Mentor Text

Grades 4–8; PB; Bio/SS

Barton, Chris. *What Do You Do with a Voice Like That? The Story of Extraordinary Congresswoman Barbara Jordan.* San Diego, CA: Beach Lane/Simon & Schuster, 2018.

What Will You Do with a Gift Like Yours?

There's a question I ask student audiences immediately after I read aloud my book *What Do You Do with a Voice Like That? The Story of Extraordinary Congresswoman Barbara Jordan.* It's a question whose answer is so easy that kids think it must be a trick.

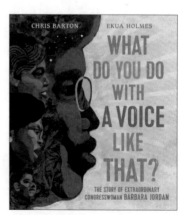

"What natural gift was Barbara Jordan born with?"

"Her voice?" they reply.

"That's right," I say. "But when Barbara Jordan was your age, did she know exactly what to do with that gift?"

They know the answer to this one, too. No, she didn't.

And it's true. This great woman whose oratorical powers inspired her constituents, brought out the best in her colleagues, and helped end Richard Nixon's shameful presidency had once possessed a talent as undeveloped as it was promising.

Just like the talents of the students I'm speaking to.

Just like my own.

I can point to the moment I got the idea to write a biography of Houston-born Jordan. It was the moment when I opened an email from fellow Texas author Kathi Appelt suggesting I do so.

But what drew me to the topic—what made Jordan's story one that I could not turn away from—came a little later.

Like many Texans, I had some idea of the basic outline of Jordan's career. I knew what they meant when they responded to her name with "Oh, I miss her" or "Oh, we need her" or "Oh, *that voice*."

Only after I started my research did I realize what, in retrospect, seems obvious: Barbara Jordan's voice was not always THE VOICE OF BARBARA JORDAN (https://bit.ly/BJSpeech). It was something that grew. Something that developed over time. Something that took shape because of efforts and choices she made, and because she heeded an inner voice that eventually took her from the halls of Congress to the front of a classroom.

It was that growth—that journey of the attribute for which she is best known—that pulled me in. I related to that.

You see, I loved writing when I was a kid. It came naturally to me. But as I ask those same student audiences today, when I was their age, did I know exactly what to do with that ability?

Again, they know the answer. And that answer would be every bit as true for me well into my twenties, when I heard my inner voice telling me to try writing books for children.

Just as Jordan grew the natural gift of her speaking voice through practice, through education, and through putting it to public use, there are things that I've since learned are essential to my development as a writer.

Chris Barton (top left) with fellow authors Jennifer Ziegler, Cynthia Levinson (bottom left), Donna Janell Bowman, and Don Tate.

Research. I couldn't write any of my nonfiction books with only the information that's already in my head.

Rewriting. Again and again and again. I figure I revise each picture book of mine, in ways large and small, on at least a hundred different days.

Collaboration. I never make a book all by myself. Besides illustrators such as Ekua Holmes, there are critique partners, editors, art directors, copy editors, and so many others.

Emphasizing all of this to my young audience sets up the question I most want those students to consider: What are *their* natural gifts, and what can they do to grow them?

Their individual talents may be as different from mine as mine is from the one that Jordan was blessed with. But the specifics of our gifts are not the point.

I want my audience to see in my personal example the same elements that I found so powerful—so compelling—in Jordan's story.

I want them to see that we all have gifts, but often we have no idea where those abilities might lead us until we begin to actively, deliberately put them to work. And I want them to see that, unless we pay attention to our own inner voices, we may not be able to fully realize—or even recognize—our own potential.

Barbara Jordan's gifts took her into the hearts of admirers across America. Mine brought me to my spot right in front of these students. Where will their gifts take them?

⊚ Carole Boston Weatherford

Carole Boston Weatherford has authored more than fifty children's books, including the Caldecott Honor winners *Freedom in Congo Square; Voice of Freedom: Fannie Lou Hamer, Spirit of the Civil Rights Movement;* and *Moses: When Harriet Tubman Led Her People to Freedom.* She is a professor of children's and adolescent literature at Fayetteville State University in North Carolina.

Nonfiction Mentor Texts

Grades 4–8; PB; Bio/SS

Weatherford, Carole Boston. *Becoming Billie Holiday.* Honesdale, PA: Wordsong, 2008.

———. *Birmingham, 1963.* Honesdale, PA: Wordsong, 2007.

———. *Freedom on the Menu: The Greensboro Sit-ins.* New York: Dial, 2004.

———. *The Legendary Miss Lena Horne.* New York: Atheneum, 2017.

———. *Moses: When Harriet Tubman Led Her People to Freedom.* New York: Hyperion, 2006.

———. *The Roots of Rap: 16 Bars on the 4 Pillars of Hip-Hop.* New York: Little Bee, 2019.

———. *Schomburg: The Man Who Built a Library.* Somerville, MA: Candlewick, 2017.

———. *Voice of Freedom: Fannie Lou Hamer, Spirit of the Civil Rights Movement.* Somerville, MA: Candlewick, 2015.

Are Kids Too Tender for Tough Topics?

Since the debut of my first children's book in 1995, I have mined the past for family stories, fading traditions, and forgotten struggles. I do so because when I was a child, Black history was not in the curriculum and few Black books were on library shelves. Not that I grew up culturally deprived—for there was always a grandmother in my house, quoting proverbs, sharing stories, passing down recipes, and humming hymns. My parents exposed me to African American culture in hopes of raising my consciousness.

That is reflected in the children's books I write. I have chronicled the Greensboro lunch counter sit-ins and the bombing of Birmingham's Sixteenth Street Baptist Church. I have profiled Underground Railroad conductor Harriet Tubman,

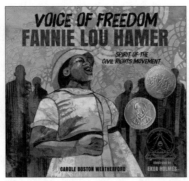

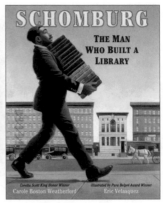

voting rights activist Fannie Lou Hamer, Harlem Renaissance bibliophile Arturo Schomburg, entertainer and civil rights activist Lena Horne, and jazz icon Billie Holiday who sang the anti-lynching hymn "Strange Fruit." My book *The Roots of Rap: 16 Bars on the 4 Pillars of Hip Hop* shows how an art form borne of disenfranchised youth and rooted in resistance evolved into a global youth culture.

I continue to focus on the African American freedom struggle. My books are often set during the slavery or Jim Crow eras. As the movement for more diverse children's books has gained steam, writing about slavery and segregation has become fraught with controversy. Debates rage about the depiction of the enslaved and about whether books with African American characters are overburdened with oppression and victimhood.

I feel strongly about the appropriateness and importance of slavery and segregation as subjects of books for young people. Of course, no child's literary diet should consist solely of tough topics. And even the youngest readers may have genre or subject preferences. But it's never too early to raise a child's consciousness, and I feel compelled to do so. Here's why.

1. Children have a more absolute sense of right and wrong—no gray areas. That's why fairy tales in which good triumphs over evil have been bedtime fixtures for generations. Likewise, social justice themes resonate with young people.

    After I read aloud books about discrimination, students invariably ask: Did that really happen? Who made that stupid rule? Why did whites mistreat Blacks? And the ringer: Which water fountain did biracial people have to use? Children demand, and we adults are obligated to offer explanations.

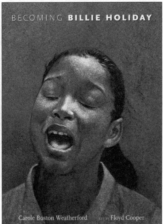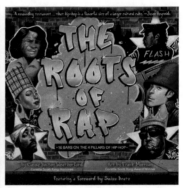

2. Children need to learn a fuller, truer history than whitewashed textbooks or bi-
    ased media provide. Children's books about the freedom struggle correct omis-
    sions and connect dots in our national narrative. By the time the Civil War began,
    four million people had been enslaved in the United States. Countless stories—
    including those of enslaved children who were forced into labor at tender ages—
    have yet to be told.

    Much history has been lost because speaking of slavery was taboo, even
    among those formerly enslaved. Similarly, memories of the Jim Crow era and
    Civil Rights Movement are fading. Gentle yet thought-provoking children's
    books such as Kelly Starling Lyons's *Ellen's Broom* and Jacqueline Woodson's *The
    Other Side* share heartwarming stories from otherwise shameful chapters in our
    nation's history.

3. Children deserve the truth, especially since racism still rears its ugly head,
    sometimes in dangerous ways. Children may not yet see race, but society
    already views them through that lens.

    African American parents have never had the luxury of raising color-
    blind children or of waiting until their children are preteens to school them
    about racism. After all, Tamir Rice was twelve years old—and playing with
    a toy gun in a Cincinnati park—when he was killed by police responding to
    a report of an armed Black man. Trayvon Martin was fourteen years old—
    and talking on his cell phone on a stroll back from the store with Skittles and
    an iced tea—when neighborhood vigilante George Zimmerman tailed him
    and shot him dead.

As long as African American victims get blamed for their own murders and African American youth are disproportionately profiled, we cannot spare children the truth. As African American parents have "the talk" with their children about how to handle a police stop, children's books about historic racism can help place police brutality along the continuum of violent oppression.

4. I write not only for African American children who may one day feel the sting of racism, but also for children growing up in households that do not foster tolerance or celebrate diversity. Unless those children read books about social justice, they risk inheriting hatred and repeating misdeeds of the past.

    I also write for educators who may have scant knowledge of African American history and heroes. After all, educators can't teach what they don't know. And children can't know what they never learn.

Slavery and segregation are inextricable from America's story. Children's books like mine preserve history and honor famous and unsung heroes. I view those books as testaments to those whose voices were muted or marginalized. My books bear witness, sparking much-needed conversations about slavery and segregation among children, parents, and educators. If we are to bridge the racial divide, our children must understand the forces that created it, and that's a responsibility I take very seriously.

⊚ Sandra Neil Wallace

 Sandra Neil Wallace is the daughter of a refugee and concentration camp survivor. A first-generation university student, she became a journalist, breaking a gender barrier in sports as the first woman to host an NHL broadcast on national TV. Sandra's books have won the Orbis Pictus Award and been selected as ALA Notables. A US citizen since 2016, Sandra advocates for social responsibility as advisor to the Cohen Center for Holocaust and Genocide Studies and cofounder of The Daily Good, a nonprofit organization bringing global food pantries to college campuses in New Hampshire.

Nonfiction Mentor Texts

Grades 4–6, 5–8; PB, LF; Bio/SS

Wallace, Sandra Neil. *Between the Lines: How Ernie Barnes Went from the Football Field to the Art Gallery.* New York: Paula Wiseman/Simon & Schuster, 2018. (Grades 4–6)

Wallace, Sandra Neil, and Rich Wallace. *First Generation: 36 Trailblazing Immigrants and Refugees Who Make America Great.* New York: Little, Brown, 2018. (Grades 5–8)

Getting at the Soul of Nonfiction Means Facing Your Fears

I have a secret to share, and it's the reason why I write nonfiction. I want to know what makes people afraid. I want to know why, despite extreme fear that may include the possibility of death, they face that fear and go on to lead brave lives.

I've come to realize that this motive is personal—that I'm looking for a blueprint on life in the hopes that I haven't strayed and can become the best human I can be. (Even though there's this fear inside me that I might fail.)

This obsession began when I realized that my family background involved trauma and the worst kinds of fear. Some of my relatives never recovered from this past. Others, despite carrying emotional scars, went on to lead fulfilling and brave lives.

That curiosity to learn and honor people who remain resilient in their quest, regardless of obstacles thrown their way, inspired me to write my first picture book biography, *Between the Lines: How Ernie Barnes Went from the Football Field to the Art Gallery.*

I'd learned of Ernie Barnes while working as a sports announcer. I never forgot his unwavering self-confidence in the face of adversity and discrimination, his strength in maintaining his identity as an artist while playing in the NFL, and his resourcefulness in navigating both worlds, refusing to adhere to stereotypes. But years after leaving ESPN, when I read that he'd died, my heart sank. Why hadn't I written about him right away? The truth was, I didn't know if I was "visual" enough to write in the picture book biography format. Instead, I spent years crafting long-form nonfiction with book lengths nearing 400 pages.

When I stumbled on an article about Ernie's artwork for the Los Angeles Olympics, I knew I had to write his story. This time, my nonfiction backlist gave me the courage to try the picture book biography format. And I soon realized that broadcast journalism had nurtured in me a deeply visual sense mechanism. I think in pictures and scenes, much like a cinematographer.

Ernie thought in pictures, too. He saw life as a canvas in motion connecting humanity. I see story as a propulsion of bold, litmus-test moments spiraling toward truth. Picture book biographies resonate with me because they form an immediate connection with the subject's soul. Writing them can often consume as much time as lengthier nonfiction because each word is weighted as heavily as a sentence or paragraph in long-form nonfiction.

In *First Generation: 36 Trailblazing Immigrants and Refugees Who Make America Great*, cowritten with Rich Wallace, the jumping-off point was my own journey toward citizenship in 2016 and the ostracization of so many immigrants and refugees with whom I took the oath during our swearing-in ceremony. I wanted their stories to be front and center, but I also needed to examine my own feelings around citizenship, being first generation and the daughter of a refugee and concentration camp survivor from the former Yugoslavia.

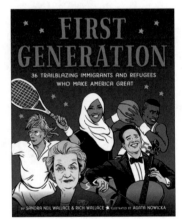

I knew right away what emotions and experiences to look for in researching our subjects, so for this book, curating was in my DNA. Yet, because this was a collective biography, we needed to achieve the heft of story through brevity and in what I call bio-sketches. To get at the core of each story, our mission statement revolved around one simple question: What is it about the person we're writing about that a child will never forget?

Photographs became a powerful and unexpected research tool. My mother cherishes the few images that my grandmother brought with them on their boat journey from Europe, and we discovered the same attachment with many of our subjects. So, for each person, we selected two moments in time or two images—like on Instagram—that defined their lives.

Growing up, I didn't talk very much about my family's traumatic past. The truth is, the laughter from my classmates when they heard my relatives speak English with heavy accents stung—a lot. But now it's a privilege to shine a light on the truth and my own life.

I know that I am who I am because of the strength and perseverance of my relatives and their unwavering will to survive, but I didn't realize that as a kid. Ultimately, *First Generation* lets first-gen kids know that they and their families are honored, valued, and appreciated. It helps forge connections and eliminate fear by showing how much we all have in common, such as the need to be safe, to belong, and to be loved.

Writing nonfiction takes courage, honesty, transparency, and a tenacity to uncover the truth. There is no hiding behind a subject. We dig deep into research and our souls and present true stories to the most valued audience on the planet: young readers.

Anita Sanchez

As a writer, Anita Sanchez is especially fascinated by plants and animals that no one loves. Her books are intended to get kids excited about the wonders of the natural world. Anita worked as an environmental educator for the New York State Department of Environmental Conservation and developed curricula for environmental science programs serving thousands of students. Many years of field work, leading children on nature walks, have given her firsthand experience in introducing students to the terrors and joys of nature.

Nonfiction Mentor Texts

Grades 4–6, 5–8; PB, LF; STEM

Sanchez, Anita. *Leaflets Three, Let It Be! The Story of Poison Ivy.* Honesdale, PA: Boyds Mills, 2015. (Grades 4–6)

————. *Rotten! Vultures, Beetles, Slime, and Nature's Other Decomposers.* Boston: Houghton Mifflin Harcourt, 2019. (Grades 5–8)

A Road Map to Nature

I sit at my desk, fidgeting and fuming. This is intolerable. I mean, I know my rights.

I gaze out the window at green fields edged with trees. The sun glows in a cloudless June sky. I can hardly sit still. They have NO RIGHT to keep me indoors on such a beautiful day. After all, third graders have rights, too.

So when the next day dawns even more alluring, I decide to take the law into my own hands. *I'm just not going to school.*

In those long-ago days, I walked to school, and on that bright spring morning, I decided to head for the woods instead of the classroom. *I'll just take the day off. No one will notice.*

Unfortunately, my bid for freedom was brief and ended, predictably, in the principal's office. My impassioned plea that it was too sunny to learn fractions was for some reason ignored.

I've never forgotten being that kid gazing out the window. And to this day, everything I write comes from that long-ago memory of longing to go outside.

Sadly, most kids these days spend very little time outside. And what time they do spend outdoors is usually on the mowed lawns of athletic fields.

Kids don't wander in the woods or climb trees or hunt for tadpoles or just mess around in nature. To many children, the outdoors is a scary place—caterpillars might be poisonous, and spiders could bite. There's even poison ivy out there.

So I set out to write books that will help kids confront their fears of the unknown. My books are set, not in a rain forest or outer space, but close to home, to create possibilities for outdoor exploration in every child's backyard or local park.

I try to encourage close-up, hands-on, get-dirty experiences. *It's okay*, I want to say to all those anxious kids standing on the blacktop. *The spider won't hurt you. This is what poison ivy looks like. It's okay.*

My book *Leaflets Three, Let It Be! The Story of Poison Ivy* highlights all the good things about, yes, poison ivy. (Did you know it's an important survival food for cardinals and bluebirds?) And it teaches kids how to identify the plant so that they can safely avoid it.

Rotten! Vultures, Beetles, Slime, and Nature's Other Decomposers focuses on stuff kids think of as disgusting or scary: fungus, tarantulas, and one of my personal favorites—slugs. At the heart of every chapter is that younger version of myself, lingering on the walk home from school to capture grasshoppers and marvel at all the amazing critters thriving under a log. I hope to persuade readers to view even the icky side of nature with curiosity and excitement. Even the grossest creepy-crawler has a place in nature's web and a fascination of its own.

With each book I write, I try to create a road map to get kids out of the house and into the backyard, or the local park, or a nearby nature center. I want them to relax and think of nature as a place that's safe, fun, and welcoming. My passion is to give young readers the knowledge to explore the outdoors safely and the confidence to stray off the sidewalk. To look closer, ask questions, get muddy.

I hope my readers will collect rocks, pick up worms, hunt for salamanders, look under rotting logs—and find an adventure that can last all their lives.

⊚ Tanya Lee Stone

Tanya Lee Stone is best known for telling unsung true stories. Her work has earned many recognitions, including an NAACP Image Award, a Sibert Medal, and a Golden Kite Award. Her books include *Courage Has No Color*; *Almost Astronauts*; *The Good, the Bad, and the Barbie*; *Who Says Women Can't Be Doctors!?*; *Elizabeth Leads the Way*; and *Pass Go and Collect $200*. *Girl Rising: Changing the World One Girl at a Time* was her one-hundredth book.

Nonfiction Mentor Texts

Grades 4–6, 5–8; LF; Bio/SS, Bio/STEM, Bio/Arts

Stone, Tanya Lee. *Almost Astronauts: 13 Women Who Dared to Dream.* Somerville, MA: Candlewick, 2009. (Grades 5–8)

———. *Sandy's Circus: A Story about Alexander Calder*. New York: Viking, 2008. (Grades 4–6)

I Tell True Stories

I am on a mission to rid us of the term *nonfiction*. It is meaning*less*. Why do we describe an entire genre of literature by what it is *NOT*? It tells us nothing about what it *IS*.

I no longer say, "I write nonfiction." Instead I say, "I tell true stories." The latter sparks excitement. Rightly so.

A true story is a real adventure. It is something that actually happened, in need of being captured, told, passed on. That's what history is, after all. A collection of true stories about ordinary people who have done extraordinarily wonderful—or horrible—things that have shaped our world. And my entire motivation for writing them comes from discovering a true story that so enthralls me I can't wait to share it with other people. (It likely also makes me an incredibly annoying dinner party guest. "Did you know that Alexander Calder *invented* the mobile?!")

Telling these stories depends on all the tools we use for fiction—character development, plot, setting, dialogue—with one crucial addition. The tool that allows me to tell an exciting story without making anything up is research. To understand the depths of this real-life character, to put myself in their shoes, to find the nuances of the plot, to become enough of an expert to do them justice, that research has to go deep. It has to get personal. Intimate, even.

Secondary sources are usually abundant, of course, but it's the primary sources that feed me. I'm especially enamored with in-person interviews and any amount of extended time I might be lucky enough to spend with a person I'm writing about.

It's in the quiet spaces, in between the formal interviews, that you have a chance to learn about a person. To watch their body language and their facial expressions in conversation, to talk about topics unrelated to your book; to *know* them. By the time I emerge from the research, the subjects I'm studying feel almost familial.

Research is another term that doesn't necessarily connote excitement. But if you call it what it really is—exploring—it takes on a whole new feel. When I think about my roots in *research*, I realize I have been doing it since I was a little girl.

Growing up on the beach in Milford, Connecticut, my sister and I conducted research every day. I mean, what else do you call calculating how long it would take to walk the long, skinny sandbar out to Charles Island before the tide might

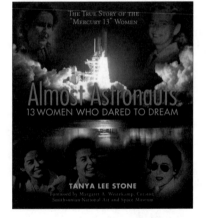

strand us there, or how much seawater we should add to the shale we just crushed in order to make a paste that could cool the sting from a jellyfish?

The things I learned then are as clear and memorable to me as the personalities and quirks of the people whose lives I have been lucky enough to *explore* in the books I have written.

In *Almost Astronauts*, for example, deep and varied research yielded me the facts, insights, and emotional information enabling me to write the opening lines to the book:

One woman stands alone, off to the side of the crowd. She paces back and forth—agitated, excited, impatient. From the back, it is hard to tell her age; her faded brown leather jacket and blond ponytail reveal nothing. But if she were to turn to glance at the group of women on the observation bleachers behind her, you would see the lines of time etched on her face. You would see a smile tinged with sadness.

It reads like fiction but is grounded in fact.

Achieving this kind of intimacy in true stories takes time. For me, it doesn't come until I am fairly far along in the writing process. My early drafts are a bit of a mess for a while, truth be told.

There's a whole lot of reading and thinking and writing and rewriting, trying to make sense of who this person really is and what is really going on in the intricacies of their life. As I revise, I dive back into the materials again and again, searching and *re-searching*.

Inevitably—and often just when I'm convinced I may never properly capture this person's story—a moment of understanding unfolds; it shows itself to me. It says: *Pay attention, this is what the story is really about, and this is why it matters to you.*

It's a difficult phenomenon to describe but unmistakable when it occurs. From that moment on, I know where I'm going. I can proceed with the business of getting what's in my head and in my heart onto the page.

◎ Kelly Milner Halls

Kelly Milner Halls began her career writing for magazines and newspapers, publishing more than one thousand articles in ten years. In 2000 she shifted her focus to children's books and has published more than fifty titles. Her best-known books are *Albino Animals, Tales of the Cryptids: Mysterious Creatures That May or May Not Exist, Death Eaters: Meet Nature's Scavengers*, and *Cryptid Creatures: A Field Guide*. Visit her at www.wondersofweird.com.

Nonfiction Mentor Texts

Grades 5–8; LF; STEM

———. *Death Eaters: Meet Nature's Scavengers.* Minneapolis, MN: Millbrook, 2018.

———. *Tales of the Cryptids: Mysterious Creatures That May or May Not Exist.* Minneapolis, MN: Millbrook, 2006.

Wonder of Weird Books

In my early years as a writer, I envied dozens of books written by other nonfiction authors. I had not yet discovered how important it is to find and cling to your inner flame—your core reason for writing.

In time, I started to ask myself, "What books did you want but never find when you were a kid?"

I was a weird little girl trapped in an era that didn't celebrate weird little girls. I loved reptiles and monsters, baseball and toads. I loved forest forts and insects, Batman and hanging out with my best friends, all boys.

After deep reflection, I realized the books I longed for then were the books I was destined to write now. Embracing the girl I was—the girl I still am—led me to my most successful path. All of my books are carefully researched, written, and revised. But they are also a little bit weird—like me.

Consider *Dinosaur Mummies*. While writing a piece for the *Chicago Tribune* on where kids could go to dig fossils, I discovered Leonardo, a fossilized duckbilled dinosaur. Most fossil finds reflect skeletal remains, but Leonardo had 70 percent of his soft tissue fossilized along with his bones. He was a mummy—amazing, and a little bit weird. The book was a huge success.

While touring the Denver Zoo, I met an African American girl with albinism—no coloring in her hair, skin, or eyes. She was remarkable—strong and bold. But I wondered what had carried her to such confidence? I wondered what I could do to support children like her. So I wrote *Albino Animals*, a celebration of a condition poorly understood. Weird.

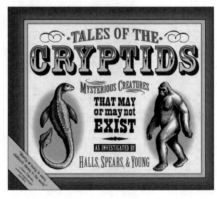

I loved watching documentaries with my father on virtually any subject. I caught fire when I saw stories of mysterious animals that might or might not be real—the creatures of cryptozoology, like Bigfoot and the Loch Ness Monster. *Tales of the Cryptids* highlighted the ideas and evidence that intrigued me as a child. And it gave weird kids like me a place to explore weird wonders of their own.

Almost every book I've published has had an element of weird and a piece of my heart, including *Death Eaters: Meet Nature's Scavengers*. When I found

a dead kitten as an eight-year-old, I brought it to my father, who helped me bury its lifeless body. I cried for hours. Then I began to wonder, "What's happening to it now?"

It took me days to confess my curiosity because I was ashamed. What kind of person would wonder about such a dark topic? But my father gave me a big hug and explained the wonders of our world's ecosystems. That sad baby cat would feed smaller creatures. Its short life would have meaning. Weird? Perhaps it is, but what a relief.

When I do school visits (and I do a LOT of them), I tell the kids that I get paid for being weird. At first, they try to be kind and defend me from such an awful label. But by the end of the hour, they are waving weird flags of their own. The word has lost its toxicity, and I am blissfully content.

Truth is, we all think we're weird. And in our own unique ways, we are. But weird is a wonder worthy of exploration. It is the thread of gold that has made my life and my career so joyful. I let kids know that they're welcome to share my core with me. Or better yet, they can dig deep and find the thread that will help them blaze a trail of their own.

© Pamela S. Turner

Pamela S. Turner was an international health consultant and policy researcher before turning to writing for children and young adults. Pamela's books, including *Hachiko, Gorilla Doctors, The Dolphins of Shark Bay, A Life in the Wild, The Frog Scientist, Samurai Rising,* and *Crow Smarts,* have won such honors as ALA Notable Book, YALSA Nonfiction Award finalist, Golden Kite Award, and the AAAS/Subaru Book Prize. Visit Pamela at www.pamelasturner.com.

Nonfiction Mentor Texts

Grades 5–8; LF; STEM

Turner, Pamela S. *Crow Smarts: Inside the Brain of the World's Brightest Bird.* Boston: Houghton Mifflin Harcourt, 2016.

———. *The Dolphins of Shark Bay.* Boston: Houghton Mifflin Harcourt, 2013.

Animalia

My first memory: reaching through the wooden bars of a playpen, trying to drag a puppy in by his ears. Although my dog-handling skills have improved, I'm still drawn to animals in a way I can't fully explain. Perhaps it's their otherness, the presence of a gulf that seems almost crossable but isn't.

As writers, our subjects often define us. I never get tired of exploring the complex, contradictory, and continually fascinating relationship we humans have with other animals.

When casting about for a subject for my first children's book, I thought: *Dog stories! I love dog stories!* The result was *Hachiko: The True Story of a Loyal Dog,* a fictionalized account of a tale I discovered while living in Tokyo. (Warning: you might want to have a tissue nearby.)

The dog was the first species domesticated and is still probably our best-beloved. Our relationship with wild animals, however, is the one I've grown most committed to probing. In *Crow Smarts: Inside the Brain of the World's Brightest Bird,* I wanted to help readers appreciate a much-maligned, underappreciated group of animals that combine astonishing intelligence and solid family values.

New Caledonian crows, the academic stars of the crow family, make and use multiple kinds of tools and on some cognitive tasks can outperform six-year-old children. This is striking evidence of convergent evolution: two groups of animals that have gone down different paths but arrived at a similar destination.

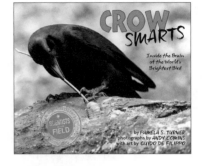

Crow Smarts was a very personal book for me because I volunteer as a wildlife rehabilitator specializing in crows and ravens. At the moment, in fact, I have a juvenile crow recuperating in my aviary after being trapped in a chimney for a week and losing about half its body weight. I have no idea how this crow got into the chimney, but intelligent animals are sometimes too curious for their own good!

Many animals, like crows, are in dire need of good PR. But a few are in need of *corrective* PR. I wrote *The Dolphins of Shark Bay* to smash a few myths about bottlenose dolphins, probably the most popular wild animal species on the planet. They perform amazing tricks! They play with swimmers! They save drowning people!—etc., etc.

In *Dolphins of Shark Bay*, I sought to show that their relationships with one another are far richer, more complex, and more interesting than their relationship

with us. We don't need to turn dolphins into noble elves in wetsuits, because these animals are astonishing enough on their own. (And by the way, as a scuba diver who has been on dives involving both sharks and dolphins, . . . I always assume Flipper's got other priorities besides "saving" me.)

I hope to continue writing books for children and young adults that strive to educate, enlighten, and entertain by putting animals in a realistic behavioral and environmental context. I hope that by doing so I'm also placing humans in a realistic context.

The famous environmentalist and myrmecologist E. O. Wilson put it best:

The more we know of other forms of life, the more we enjoy and respect ourselves. Humanity is exalted not because we are so far above other living creatures, but because knowing them well elevates the very concept of life.*

Biophilia: The Human Bond with Other Species by E. O. Wilson, Harvard University Press, Boston, 1984, p. 22.

 Karen Romano Young

Karen Romano Young frequently goes into the field with scientists to tell their stories in words and pictures. Her explorations include the frozen Arctic Ocean, Antarctica, the Galapagos Islands, and the East Pacific Rise (two miles deep in the ocean). She writes nonfiction, graphic nonfiction, fiction, and graphic novels for children and is the creator of science comics about exploration and research. Find her at karenromanoyoung.com.

Nonfiction Mentor Texts

Grades 5–8; LF; STEM

Young, Karen Romano. *Antarctica: The World's Shrinking Continent.* London: What on Earth, 2021.

———. #AntarcticLog, antarcticlog.com.

———. *Try This! 50 Fun Experiments for the Mad Scientist in You.* Washington, DC: National Geographic, 2014.

———. *Try This! Extreme: 50 Fun & Safe Experiments for the Mad Scientist in You.* Washington, DC: National Geographic, 2017.

The Invitation

Being included—being told *you can do this, you can be here, you should be here*—is what gets kids engaged and involved in science right now, and for life. When it comes to science, I don't believe enough people of any age are hearing this message. In my science writing, my goal is to make kids feel invited, included, involved, and validated, no matter how inexperienced they may be.

When I was a child, my life was full of adults who let me tag along. I learned how to grow rhubarb, hang bookshelves, shop for fabric/screws/

used cars/tomatoes, change the oil on a lawnmower, shuffle cards, dress a wound, cut off the circulation to a skin mole, body surf, determine whether the tide was coming in or going out, plant bulbs, take off and land an airplane, build a treehouse, train a dog, curl hair, scramble eggs, kill mildew, care for a stunned bird, fix my glasses, hunt for fiddlehead ferns, find secrets in a painting, saw a bottle in half, wire a lamp, and much, much, much more.

Sometimes trying these things made me feel shaky—too dumb, unskilled, or inexperienced. And the fact is, I screwed up continually. But the experts in my life (merely people who were a few steps ahead of me) helped me through my most vulnerable moments. They made being shaky okay.

Through my research, participation in lab work and fieldwork, writing and drawing, I've learned that my ability to mirror kids' feelings of being dumb, disengaged/bored, or excluded—and flip them to simply being *shaky because they're new to something*—is my most valuable offering.

It's the degree to which people are willing to plow past these shaky feelings that makes the difference in their success as learners—whether that person is a kid, a PhD scientist, or a middle-aged author. If the question is "Do I belong here?" then the answer must be "Come on in."

The answer lies in the invitation, and in the way it's given. If I could, I'd invite every reader to personally accompany me on a science adventure. We'd talk along the way, and if we made enough mistakes, we'd find the right way.

One frozen March morning, I climbed aboard an icy boat in Antarctica to assist Pete Countway, a Bigelow Laboratory for Ocean Sciences molecular biologist. Pete had offered to bring me along for two months as his lab assistant in exchange for my creating science comics about his work.

Before the trip, I must have told him six times that I didn't know how to do lab work, had only helped with fieldwork before, and shouldn't be put in charge of anything important. . . .

This brilliant scientist said, "It'll be okay."

And it was, until I turned on the water pump and flooded the lab. Sure enough, I'd screwed up. Who doesn't know the shaky feeling I had in my stomach?

I ran to find Pete, and *he* apologized: it wasn't my fault, he said; he hadn't shown me how to empty "the pig," a big jar into which waste water ran, so the pig (not I) had made the mess.

I was nervous all over again when we went to sea to capture water samples. I had to learn a whole new process, one involving heavy lifting, deft maneuvering, and quick thinking, aboard a pitching, freezing boat, in the snow.

But then I watched Pete learn to do something that made him feel shaky—operating the boat's winch, which involved a sticky knob, adjustments for the height of waves, and a sharp eye on the angle of the A-frame used to lift our instruments into the Southern Ocean.

"You're going to have to allow me a little learning curve here," he told Andrew, who was running the boat.

Andrew laughed and shrugged. He had only just recently learned his way around the winch himself. It's great when people can articulate their inexperience and need for a little leeway, but then jump in and try anyway.

Writing about science for children is full of moments when I think they could get the shakes—feel intimidated or uninvited—just when I most want them to be engaged, excited, and to think, "This is for me." I want them to see their role in the science story.

When I say that feeling dumb is my superpower, that's what I'm talking about. I try to channel my own sense of inadequacy or ignorance and to share with kids what's useful and essential about those feelings, to set an example of how to deal with them.

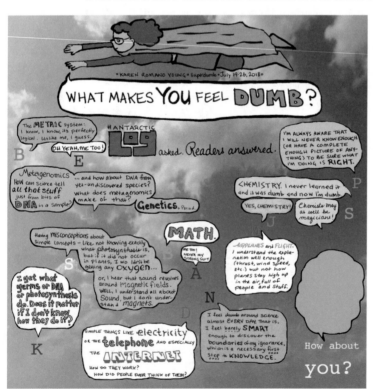

I believe that kids are born curious, born wanting to see and know and do. When they read about smart scientists or foolish artists having adventures, it's the same as watching a parent or friend do a task: they want to learn how and to be involved.

They must not be shooed away by feeling dumb or shaky because they don't see how to get where they want to go. The message must always be: you are fine, you are wanted, I'll show you the way.

⊚ Jennifer Swanson

Jennifer Swanson is the award-winning author of more than forty nonfiction books for children. Using the background in science and history that she received from the US Naval Academy and her MS in education, Jennifer excels in making complex facts accessible, compelling, and humorous for young readers. She is the creator of the *STEM Tuesday* blog and has presented at numerous conferences, the World Science Festival, and the Library of Congress's National Book Festival. Find Jennifer at www.JenniferSwansonBooks.com.

Nonfiction Mentor Texts

Grades 5–8; LF; STEM

Swanson, Jennifer. *Astronaut-Aquanaut: How Space Science and Sea Science Interact*. Washington, DC: National Geographic, 2018.

————. *Brain Games: The Mind-Blowing Science of Your Amazing Brain*. Washington, DC: National Geographic, 2015.

————. *Super Gear: Nanotechnology and Sports Team Up*. Watertown, MA: Charlesbridge, 2016.

Lifelong Science Lover

For as long as I can remember, I have loved science. Curiosity about the world has fueled my passions throughout my life.

Some of my earliest memories are examining grass and flowers under a magnifying glass and climbing trees to see things up close. It makes perfect sense that I started a science club in my garage when I was seven years old.

I was always asking questions. "Why does *this* tree grow so tall but the one next to it doesn't?" "Why does *this* flower have five petals but that one has fifty?" "Why does my brother have brown eyes but my eyes are green?"

I probably drove my parents and teachers nuts with all my questions. But the drive to understand how the world works, how everything fits together, is deep inside me. It's central to both my personal and writing life.

My quest to discover how things work led me to major in chemistry at the US Naval Academy, where I also learned engineering and technology. I was hooked! It's probably why many of the topics I write about tend toward the "-TEM" part of STEM.

As I was writing *Brain Games: The Mind-Blowing Science of Your Amazing Brain*, I wanted to know, "How does the brain work?" That's a simple question, but one with a complicated answer. So I broke up each chapter into smaller questions: *How does your brain think? How do memories and emotions work? How does your brain make your body move?*

For most people, science is best learned through *doing*, not just reading, so each chapter includes awesome activities that *show* the reader how their brain works. Including activities and experiments in my books comes naturally. It reminds me of my many days as a kid working with the boxed chemistry labs that I got for my birthdays.

One of my most recent titles stemmed from a question I had during a conversation with my editor. We were talking about how astronauts train, and I wondered if aquanauts train the same way. After all, space and the deep ocean are sort of similar environments, aren't they?

WOW! What a question. I had to find out.

I dove deep into research (something I love), and the result was *Astronaut-Aquanaut: How Space Science and Sea Science Interact*. This is one of my favorite books because it's the culmination of my long-held curiosity about both space and the ocean.

My two childhood heroes were Jacques Cousteau, the famous oceanographer, and Sally Ride, the first female US astronaut. At certain times in my life, I wanted to be either or both of them. While writing this book, my research took me UP into space (like Sally Ride) and DOWN into the ocean (like Jacques Cousteau) as I learned the fascinating answers to (almost) all of my questions.

Like most curious people, I don't limit myself to certain topics. I ask questions about pretty much everything—from the emptiness of space and the vast ocean to the tiny structures that make nanotechnology possible.

Nanotechnology is the science of the microscopic. It's used to create some of the strongest materials on the planet . . . and almost every kind of sports equipment you can think of!

Growing up in a household with three brothers and a father who loved sports, I succumbed to the inevitable and ended up playing and loving sports myself. It's a deep-seated love born out of many hours spent watching my brothers' baseball games, football games, and golf matches. But it's also the result of my own experiences running track, swimming, and (trying to) play softball.

My love of sports and my desire to know how things work merged during the 2008 Olympic Games. When Michael Phelps and his teammates debuted full-body swimsuits and proceeded to break more than 125 records, I was fascinated. I wanted to know *how* they did that. Research led me to nanotechnology, and the result was *Super Gear: Nanotechnology and Sports Team Up*.

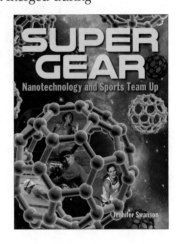

If you pick up one of my books, you will inevitably find that it answers a BIG question. One that I have about how the world works, one that I hope my readers have, too. As I'm writing, I imagine my seven-year-old self, with that microscope in my garage, discovering new and wondrous things. I put that same sense of accomplishment, the joy of figuring things out, into each book I write.

 Elizabeth Partridge

Elizabeth Partridge writes about rough times and brave, complicated people. Her books include *Restless Spirit: The Life and Work of Dorothea Lange* and *Marching for Freedom*. She has received the *Los Angeles Times* Book Prize, a Printz Honor Book, and the Boston Globe–Horn Book Award. *This Land Was Made for You and Me* was a National Book Award finalist, and *Boots on the Ground* was longlisted for the National Book Award.

Nonfiction Mentor Texts

Grades 7–8; LF; Bio/SS, SS

Partridge, Elizabeth. *Boots on the Ground: America's War in Vietnam*. New York: Viking, 2018.

———. "Nightly News." In Marc Aronson and Susan Campbell Bartoletti (Eds.), *1968: Today's Authors Explore a Year of Rebellion, Revolution, and Change*. Somerville, MA: Candlewick, 2018.

My Anguish about the Vietnam War and Why I Keep Writing about It

Since I was a teenager, I've been haunted by the Vietnam War. During high school and college, I was passionately against the war. I hated the suffering, death, and destruction the war brought. My heart broke for the Vietnamese, for the Americans sent to fight, and for our torn, divided country.

After the war, protestors and returning vets didn't mix. Veterans came home, let their hair grow long, and tried to blend in. I heard a few stories, but only scraps. I wondered, how had the young Americans fared when they came back home? I explored the idea by writing a historical fiction novel, *Dogtag Summer*. I filled my mind with research and set up a difficult premise: what happens when a Vietnam veteran adopts an Amerasian girl from Vietnam and their PTSD is suddenly triggered and tears the family apart?

With historical fiction, I needed to know the history of the period. I needed to have a realistic setting and characters who would act within the bounds of the past. But I was free to make up the characters and plot out their lives.

I finished the manuscript and told my husband that even if I never wrote another word I'd be happy.

That lasted for a few days.

The Vietnam War tapped on my shoulder again. The Americans who served, the real ones, what was it like for them to fight in the war? To be trained to kill, to fight, to lose friends in battle? This time I wanted to write narrative nonfiction—also called creative or literary nonfiction—to tell a true story, using real people. No making anything up: no weather, no dialogue, no clothing, no thoughts. Nothing. It took me six years.

I began by doing a deep dive, reading much more about the war. Gradually I focused on what really interested me, looking especially at primary source materials: oral histories, recordings, photographs, and documents. Then I set out to find veterans to interview from different parts of the country and from different ethnic groups to see how race played out in their experiences.

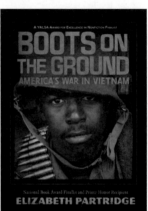

For *Boots on the Ground: America's War in Vietnam*, I interviewed six men who had fought in the war, a nurse, and a refugee, and then wove their interview chapters with alternating chapters on presidents and protestors. In every chapter, I added photographs. I love this place as a writer: up close, my nose pressed against the glass. Words, direct from people who were there, and photographs resonate with information and emotion.

Just as I was finishing the book, Susan Campbell Bartoletti asked me if I would contribute to the anthology she and Marc Aronson were editing, *1968: Today's Authors Explore a Year of Rebellion, Revolution, and Change*. Something, she said, about 1968 that really has stuck with you.

I said no. Thanks, but just . . . no. I was done with 1968 and the war and the protests. I'd already written a prologue for *Boots on the Ground* where I recounted several of my experiences in high school and as an adult, and what led to my urgent need to write a nonfiction book on the war.

But Susan is persuasive, and she knows me really well. You could, she said casually, write something memoir-style. Maybe a prose poem.

I'd never written a long prose poem. And Susan knows I love a good challenge.

A prose poem about my life would be memoir writing, which some people consider to be a subgenre of narrative nonfiction, but others consider it to stand alongside narrative nonfiction, its own genre of nonfiction. *Brown Girl Dreaming* by Jacqueline Woodson is a terrific example of a young adult prose poem.

Memoir writing is more subjective than narrative nonfiction, told directly from the author's perspective. It's more raw, more supple, more intense. It's all true—at least from the author's perspective. Often in memoirs there is dialogue. It's unlikely they were the exact words spoken, but they are true to the spirit of the conversation.

I found, in the boiled-down prose poem I wrote, "Nightly News," the essence of my own anguished feelings during the war. And by writing in all three genres, I've finally explored everything I need to say about the Vietnam War.

Sorting out these different genres can be challenging. To clarify which genre you are reading or writing, or to help your students, ask a few questions. Is it a real time and place, but the characters are from the writer's imagination? That's historical fiction. Are the characters real people, but they say and do things the writer made up? Still historical fiction. Real people, real times, real places with nothing made up? Narrative nonfiction. Told from the point of view of the writer about their own life, the way they remember it happening? Memoir.

Each genre is strong and powerful. Each one is a wonderful challenge. Enjoy!

In the Classroom

As you read the mentor essays in this chapter, you probably noticed that, in some cases, professional writers start with a specific focus in mind. For example, Barb Rosenstock's biographies don't begin with a person. They start with an idea, memory, or experience that has meaning for her, and she uses that personal connection to focus her writing.

Jess Keating, Traci Sorell, Carole Boston Weatherford, Sandra Neil Wallace, Anita Sanchez, Kelly Milner Halls, Karen Romano Young, and Pamela S. Turner return to the same focus again and again. Their writing has a central theme, a mission, a purpose that they feel driven to explore and share with their readers. If students use the Idea Incubator strategy described in Chapter 1 (see pages 60–61) for an extended period of time, they may be able to take a similar approach to finding a focus for their writing.

According to Elizabeth Partridge's essay, she is so obsessed with a single topic—the Vietnam War—that she has written about it three times, each time using a different genre to focus her exploration. If you have students who are *really* enthusiastic about a particular topic, they might enjoy trying something similar.

But not all authors begin each new book with a specific focus in mind. Like many young writers, finding a focus is part of their creative process. Here are some of the strategies they use.

Strategy 1: Start with a Question

As you learned at the beginning of this chapter, *A Seed Is the Start* began with a question. When I saw a Pinterest board with an incredible variety of seeds, I asked myself: "How does a seed's external features contribute to its ability to survive and germinate?" That question focused my thinking and helped me target my research.

Questions also help guide Laura Purdie Salas and Jennifer Swanson in early stages of the writing process. Laura's favorite question is "What else?" She asks it again and again as she shapes the ideas and information her manuscript will explore.

Jennifer is a curious person who is always asking questions. Her books often begin with a BIG question, but she also asks herself dozens of smaller questions as she organizes information and searches for the best way to present her topic to her young audience.

If you've adopted some of the strategies included in Chapter 1, students should already have questions they can use as a starting point. Encourage them to look for questions that interest them on the classroom Idea Board or their Idea Incubator lists. They can also brainstorm questions about some of the amazing things they've been noticing around them. Students can use these questions to guide their research.

Not only does this approach guarantee that students will have some skin in the game, but a specific query will lead to more targeted note taking. It will also give students authentic opportunities to make connections between information they find in a variety of sources.

Strategy 2: Look for the "Oh, wow!"

Wouldn't it be wonderful if writers could always identify their focus at the beginning of the prewriting process? Unfortunately, that often isn't the case. Sometimes writers have to be in the thick of things before their focus becomes clear.

What should writers do when they begin researching with nothing more than a general topic in mind? Author Deborah Heiligman (whose essay is included in Chapter 3) recommends a targeted note-taking strategy in which students read broadly about their topic and jot down only information that makes them say, "Oh, wow!" This approach helps writers view the topic through their own lens and pinpoint the ideas and information that interest them most.

This is literally what Jason Chin did as he was creating *Grand Canyon*. After reading widely about his topic without a specific approach in mind, Jason decided to visit the canyon. And the first time he walked up to the edge, he had an "Oh, wow!" experience that inspired him and guided his creative process as he wrote and illustrated the book.

When Deborah employs her "Oh, wow!" technique, she uses the notes she has taken to develop a "mantra"—a statement that helps her determine what information to highlight and what to leave out. She writes the statement on a piece of paper and tapes it to the wall above her computer.

Barbara Kerley describes a similar process in her essay. Whether she's writing a picture book biography with a narrative writing style or a concept book with an expository writing style, she creates a sentence that focuses her thinking and her writing.

Chris Barton may not have written down the mantra that guided him as he wrote *What Do You Do with a Voice Like That? The Story of Extraordinary Congresswoman Barbara Jordan*, but his essay clearly explains how a core idea that emerged during his research process helped him focus his manuscript *and* fueled his passion for the project.

Strategy 3: Thought Prompts

Unfortunately, a focus doesn't always solidify in a writer's mind while they are researching. At the beginning of the chapter, I described how my focus for *Can an Aardvark Bark?* emerged only after I had written many, many drafts. Tanya Lee Stone describes a similar experience in her essay. It was the act of writing and rewriting that eventually allowed Tanya to understand what *Almost Astronauts: 13 Women Who Dared to Dream* was *really* about and why that mattered to her.

While it's hard for a writer to second-guess their process after the fact, I suspect that I wouldn't have struggled quite so much with *Can an Aardvark Bark?* if I'd used a fantastic strategy I later learned from Ryan Scala, a fifth-grade teacher in East Hampton, New York.

When students are done researching, Ryan encourages them to review their notes and circle facts and ideas they consider especially important or interesting. Then he invites them to choose one of the following prompts and jot some thoughts in their writer's notebook:

- The idea this gives me . . .
- I was surprised to learn . . .
- This makes me think . . .
- This is important because . . .

I decided to try this technique while writing *Ick! Delightfully Disgusting Animal Dinners, Dwellings, and Defenses.* I knew I wanted to include a 100-word section about flesh flies in the book, but I wasn't sure what to focus on. I had so much great gross information:

- Some flesh flies drink juices from rotting fruit. Many sip liquids from animal poop and animal carcasses.
- Some female flesh flies place their worm-like maggots (larvae) on dung. Others choose rotting carcasses or the open wounds of living animals.
- Some flesh fly maggots burrow into live animals, including other insects, snails, and toads.
- Some flesh fly maggots eat their hosts from the inside out and eventually kill them.

I could have tried to cram all this information into the book, but I knew that would be a mistake. Anytime writers use too many general words like *some* and *many*, the writing gets less interesting. I wanted my writing to be lively and full of fascinating, specific details.

But I was having trouble deciding what to highlight, and I felt overwhelmed. So I searched through my notes for Ryan's four-thought prompts. Then I reviewed my research, chose a prompt, and jotted the following in my writer's notebook:

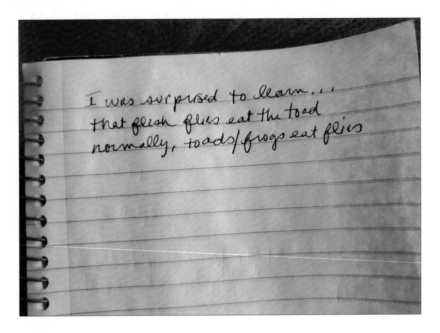

Until I wrote that sentence on paper, I hadn't really thought about the irony of a fly eating a toad. I decided that would be a fun focus, so I did some more research to learn as much as I could about the flesh fly species that targets toads. Then I eagerly wrote about their unusual relationship.

Why is finding a focus of personal interest so important to the nonfiction writing process? It forces writers to be specific, and it helps them stay engaged, both of which result in prose that's interesting and unique. I'd recommend trying one or more of these strategies with your class the next time they write nonfiction.

Making It Personal

Getting Started

In November 2016, author Sarah Albee and I developed a presentation called "Helping Students Overcome Their Biggest Nonfiction Writing Roadblocks" for a nErDcamp conference at Jericho Middle School on Long Island, New York.

At the start of the session, we asked attendees—a mix of school librarians, literacy educators, and classroom teachers—to brainstorm a list of common challenges their students face as they write nonfiction. After recording the group's responses on chart paper, Sarah and I suggested solutions based on our experience as professional writers.

Most of the challenges attendees mentioned were no surprise to us. Some were craft based, such as experimenting with text structures and adding voice to nonfiction writing. Others were more procedural, such as developing strategies for effective note taking and organizing research. And, of course, the educators were looking for advice on how to convince students to revise. Sarah and I were ready with tips and tools for addressing all of these roadblocks.

But attendees also mentioned one challenge that caught us off guard—plagiarism. We had a fascinating whole-group discussion about this roadblock, but no one could offer a clear solution.

Because the presentation went so well, Sarah and I repeated it at several other conferences. Again and again, plagiarism appeared on teachers' lists of significant roadblocks. Clearly, this was an aspect of nonfiction writing that needed to be addressed. Why do students who know they shouldn't copy their sources do it anyway? And why don't the professional writers I know feel that same temptation?

The answer to these questions suddenly became clear to me during the 2017 NCTE Annual Convention presentation I mentioned in the introduction of this book. Professional nonfiction writers don't plagiarize because we put a piece of ourselves into our writing. We analyze and synthesize our research notes to make our own meaning. Many students don't take the time or don't have the skills to make a personal connection to the information they've collected. In other words, their prewriting process is missing a critical step.

In some cases, professional nonfiction writers add a gigantic piece of themselves to their prose. For example, the opening lines of my book *Pipsqueaks, Slowpokes, and Stinkers: Celebrating Animal Underdogs* popped into my mind as I was lying in bed on a chilly December morning, waiting for the alarm to go off:

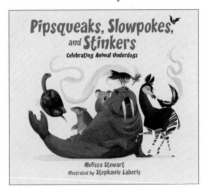

> Everyone loves elephants. They're so big and strong.
>
> Everyone respects cheetahs. They're so fast and fierce.
>
> But this book isn't about them. It's about the unsung underdogs of the animal world. Don't you think it's time someone paid attention to them?

I jumped out of bed, ran to my desk, and scrawled those lines in my writer's notebook. I couldn't believe it. In one flash of inspiration, I had the book's introduction and its hook and its voice. It felt like a gift from the universe, and it was. But it came with a catch.

As I typed the words into a computer file later that morning, I realized that a dark part of my subconscious was rearing its ugly head. That creative hook, that unique perspective, hadn't just come out of nowhere. It was born out of the severe bullying I'd endured as a child. I suddenly realized that writing the book would mean revisiting some painful memories, and that scared me.

So I shut the computer file, and I didn't open it again for six months. By that time, I'd made peace with the part of my past that would drive the creation of this book. And I got to work . . . because that's what writers do.

In the end, my personal connection made *Pipsqueaks, Slowpokes, and Stinkers* a book about animal adaptations *and* celebrating the oftentimes underappreciated traits that make us different and unique. It's my way of offering hope to children who are being bullied right now.

As you read the mentor essays in this chapter, you'll see that my story of digging deep isn't unique. To craft engaging nonfiction, writers need to be personally invested.

Luckily, that doesn't always require plunging into our past vulnerabilities whole hog. Any kind of emotional connection can supply the creative spark that brings nonfiction writing to life. For example, for *Ick! Delightfully Disgusting Animal Dinners, Dwellings, and Defenses*, the book I discussed at the end of Chapter 2, I added a much smaller piece of myself, making it a manageable model for young writers.

After using a thought prompt (see page 115) to develop a focus for the double-page spread about flesh flies, I kept noodling around in my writer's notebook. I was trying to think of creative ways to present the information. Here are some notes I made:

I thought it might be possible to use a humorous voice and somehow incorporate the word *croak*, which has a double meaning. After writing down the second phrase, I noticed the words *the end* and thought that perhaps I could use a narrative writing style.

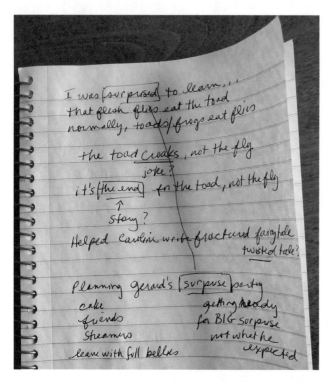

As I continued brainstorming, I started to make personal connections. My notes about possibly sharing the information as a story made me think about helping my niece write a fractured fairy tale for school. Maybe I could write a sort of twisted tale about the flesh fly.

As I reread my notes, the word *surprised* made me think of the party I had recently planned for my husband. Maybe the surprising nature of the fly-toad relationship should be the central idea of the piece.

Because I'd come up with two different ways to approach the text and I liked them both, I decided to create two different pieces and then figure out which one I liked better.

Version 1: A Toad-al Surprise

Think you know what happens when a fly and a toad cross paths? Then get ready for a BIG surprise!

When a female flesh fly encounters a harlequin toad, she doesn't become lunch. Instead, she darts down and deposits her newly hatched maggots on the toad's skin.

What happens next? The white, wormy youngsters get to work, burrowing into the toad's body. Then the maggots devour their victim from the inside out.

That's right. In this scenario, it's the toad that croaks.

Version 2: The Fly and the Toad

Once upon a time, there was a fly and a toad. Think you know how this story ends? Think again.

In this twisted tale, a female flesh fly deposits her newly hatched larvae on a harlequin toad's skin. The white, wormy youngsters wriggle and squirm as they burrow into the toad's body. Then the maggots devour their victim from the inside out.

The end.

Actually, it's the end for the toad, but not for the larvae. With their bellies full, the maggots turn into pupae. And a few weeks after that, they emerge as adults.

If you look closely at these two versions, you can see how they connect to the ideas I explored in my writer's notebook. You'll also notice that some phrases appear in both pieces. This is the factual information that came from my research.

Because I took the time to find a focus and make a personal connection, I was able to create two pieces that are different from each other and different from the way another writer would describe the fly-toad relationship. Not only does this method for evaluating and synthesizing research make the writing more vibrant and interesting, it also helps writers avoid plagiarism.

So which version did I end up using in my book? If you look at the section about flesh flies on pages 68–69 of *Ick!*, you'll find text very close to Version 1. But if you turn to the section about bombardier beetles on pages 94–95 (shown below), you'll see some similarities to Version 2. So, in a way, I ended up using them both.

There are three things to take away from this anecdote:

1. Personal connections make nonfiction writing engaging and unique.
2. Even small moments from our lives can help us create nonfiction writing that shines.
3. No writing is ever wasted.

Essays by Mentor Authors

Now that you know a little bit about how I add a piece of myself to my writing, I encourage you to take a look at what some other authors have to say about making their writing personal. After all, there's no single right way to go about this or any other step in the nonfiction writing process. Every writer does things a little bit differently, and that's an important message for students to hear.

If you have time, you may want to read all seventeen essays, but if not, Teacher Timesaver Table 3.1 will help you identify the ones that are of greatest value to you right now.

TEACHER TIMESAVER TABLE 3.1. A Guide to Mentor Essays about Making Personal Connections

Author	Grade Level	Book Format*	Content Area*	Essay Highlights
Jennifer Ward	4–5	PB	STEM	Jennifer draws on a lifetime of curiosity, wonder, and personal experiences as she forms thoughts and places them on paper.
Heather Lang	4–5	PB	Bio/SS	The women Heather writes about have fueled her personal growth, inspiring her to take risks and embrace failure.
April Pulley Sayre	4–5	PB	STEM	In her essay, April asks: "How could writing and illustrating nonfiction *not* be personal?" She sees writing as sharing her love of the real world with others.
Baptiste Paul	4–6	PB	Bio/SS, SS	Baptiste's childhood experiences of living in poverty on St. Lucia inform his writing, allowing him to present information richly and accurately.
Seth Fishman	4–6	PB	STEM	Seth wrote *A Hundred Billion Trillion Stars* for his son, hoping it would "ignite a sense of wonder about things we don't understand and convey the idea that it's okay to not know."
Stephen R. Swinburne	4–5, 5–8	PB, LF	STEM	Stephen's personal experience observing a female sea turtle lay eggs inspired him to write three books about the amazing marine reptiles.
Deborah Heiligman	4–5, 5–8, 7–8	PB, LF	Bio/SS, Bio/STEM, STEM	As Deborah wrote *From Caterpillar to Butterfly*, her work was fueled by personal connections to her son, her recently deceased mother, and her childhood self.
Candace Fleming	4–6, 5–8	PB, LF	Bio/SS, STEM	Candace says, "[T]he true tales I write spring directly from my experiences, passions, heartbreaks, obsessions, fears, quirks, curiosities, beliefs, desires. Writing nonfiction is like sitting before a blank screen and scraping off a piece of myself."
Cynthia Levinson	4–6, 5–8, 6–8	PB, LF	Bio/SS, SS	Cynthia's essay explains how writing nonfiction allows her to explore and share her curiosities, passions, concerns, and values with young readers.

Laurie Ann Thompson	4–6, 5–8, 7–8	PB, LF	Bio/SS, How-to, STEM/SS	Laurie struggled to write *Emmanuel's Dream* for years, until she thought deeply about her personal connection to the story. Adding a piece of herself to the manuscript brought the writing to life.
Donna Janell Bowman	4–8	PB	Bio/SS	Donna says, "After researching the dickens out of my subjects, my inner storyteller frames a narrative through the lens of my own life experiences."
Patricia Newman	4–8	LF	STEM	According to Patricia, "[M]y books meet an emotional need within me." They focus on themes that "light *my* fire with a personal connection."
Paula Yoo	4–6, 7–8	PB, LF	Bio/Arts, Bio/SS, Bio/Sports	The painful racism Paula experienced as a child and teenager inspire her to chronicle the important contributions of Asian Americans.
Nancy F. Castaldo	4–8, 5–8, 7–8	LF	STEM	Nancy's essay highlights her childhood and family connections to the books she chooses to write as an adult.
Lee Wind	5–8	LF	Bio/SS	When Lee was growing up, he felt alone and ashamed. He wrote *No Way, They Were Gay?* so today's LGBTQ+ youth won't have to hide their inner truth.
Heather L. Montgomery	5–8	LF	STEM	Heather's essay describes how her lifelong passion for inquiry formed the foundation for writing *Something Rotten: A Fresh Look at Roadkill*.
Carla Killough McClafferty	6–8	LF	Bio/SS, Bio/STEM	In her essay, Carla provides examples of how she uses the fire of her emotions to write about topics that fascinate her in unique and engaging ways.

*Key to Abbreviations
Book Format: PB = picture book, LF = long form
Content Area: Bio = biography, SS = social studies/history, STEM = science/technology/engineering/math

After you've read the essays that seem best suited to your current needs, please turn to the In the Classroom section that begins on page 172. It provides a variety of practical ideas that can help you support students as they add a piece of themselves to the nonfiction they write.

⑥ Jennifer Ward

Jennifer Ward is the award-winning author of more than twenty books for children, most influenced by science and nature, including *Mama Dug a Little Den*, illustrated by Steve Jenkins; *Feathers and Hair, What Animals Wear*, illustrated by Jing Jing Tsong; and *What Will Grow?*, illustrated by Susie Ghahremani, which received three starred reviews. She is easily distracted by everything outside her windows. Find her at www.JenniferWardBooks.com.

Nonfiction Mentor Texts

Grades 4–5; PB; STEM

Ward, Jennifer. *How to Find a Bird*. San Diego: Beach Lane/Simon & Schuster, 2020.

———. *I Love Birds! 52 Ways to Wonder, Wander, and Explore Birds with Kids*. Boulder, CO: Roost Books, 2019.

———. *Mama Built a Little Nest*. San Diego: Beach Lane/Simon & Schuster, 2014.

About a Bird

"Write what you know." It's a phrase often shared to encourage students with their writing process. I am a firm believer in "write what you know," having been a teacher and someone who now writes full-time for a living.

As writers we pull from the innate "what we know" to form thoughts and place them on paper. This applies to any genre of writing, be it poetry, fiction, or nonfiction. This innate knowledge forms individually from a lifetime filled with curiosity, wonder, and personal experiences. It seems I have always been curious about animals, specifically birds, so it's no wonder they often surface in my writing.

One of my earliest books involved trying to better understand bird feathers. I sorted and classified feathers that our pet parakeets, Linus and Benji, had shed, carefully organizing them and gluing them to stapled pages of construction paper.

I also learned early on that it's not easy to make a bird's nest. My first attempt took place when I was a child, perhaps age five. I was determined to build one and spent hours gathering cut, dried grass from the mowed lawn in our suburban neighborhood. I wet it in water runoff trickling down our street and formed nest after nest by squishing the grass together in small, circular shapes.

I discovered that water is indeed cohesive, but once my nests dried, they fell apart and the grass blew away. Birds clearly had the upper hand (or beak, so to speak) when it came to engineering nests.

I suppose I've always had that "Huh!" thought regarding birds and nest building, because I simply could not give up on the idea. As an adult, when a hummingbird built her tiny cup nest outside my kitchen window, I watched her for weeks as the nest formed, bit by tiny bit. I knew then that I had to dig deeper into avian architecture, and the idea for *Mama Built a Little Nest* was born.

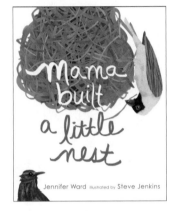

As a child, I was told that if I sprinkled salt on a bird's tail, I could catch it and it wouldn't fly away. I was enchanted by the idea of a wee, wild bird, content to be my friend, perched complacently on my finger, both of us glad of each other's company.

So at the age of six, I crouched quietly for hours at the base of a tree, salt shaker in hand, hoping a bird would hop by on the ground. And several did, but I was never stealthy enough with the salt shaker to prove the salt-to-tail theory true.

But those memories likely planted the seed for my book *How to Find a Bird*, which explains that we need not always look up to spot birds. They can also be found down low.

And my lifelong fascination with birds is clearly the inspiration behind *I Love Birds! 52 Ways to Wonder, Wander, and Explore Birds with Kids*. To this day, I spend hours with birds in the wild—observing them, wondering about them, getting inspired by them.

All writers, including nonfiction writers, create work that's deeply rooted in the personal experiences and memories that shape who and what we are. Those experiences form beliefs and fuel passions. They invite us to question and wonder, and they ignite our creativity.

I hope the books I write for children stimulate readers to dig deeper themselves to explore the many layers of nature and science, so that they, too, may think, "Huh!"

⊚ Heather Lang

Heather Lang loves to write about real women who overcame extraordinary obstacles and never gave up on their dreams. Her research adventures have taken her to the skies, the treetops of the Amazon, and the depths of the ocean. Heather's award-winning picture book biographies include *Fearless Flyer: Ruth Law and her Flying Machine*; *Queen of the Track: Alice Coachman, Olympic High-Jump Champion*; and *The Original Cowgirl: The Wild Adventures of Lucille Mulhall.* Visit her at www .heatherlangbooks.com.

Nonfiction Mentor Texts

Grades 4–5; PB; Bio/SS

Lang, Heather. *Anybody's Game: Kathryn Johnston, the First Girl to Play Little League Baseball.* Chicago: Albert Whitman, 2018.

———. *Fearless Flyer: Ruth Law and Her Flying Machine.* Honesdale, PA: Boyds Mills/ Calkins Creek, 2016.

———. *Swimming with Sharks: The Daring Discoveries of Eugenie Clark.* Chicago: Albert Whitman, 2016.

Experience It! Nonfiction Writing as a Personal Journey

Writing nonfiction is a highly personal experience for me—a journey. And the adventure always begins with a strong connection to my topic. While the connection could be rooted in passion, it might also stem from intense curiosity . . . or fear.

And what better way to explore a topic than through the experiences of brave women from history? As a child and young adult, I often avoided trying new things because I feared failure.

But now I realize how important failure is to growth and success. The women I write about inspire me to take risks and embrace failure. This often involves taking on challenging and exciting hands-on research so I can truly understand who and what I am writing about.

I grow personally with every book I write. Here are a few examples of how this has played out.

The spark for *Fearless Flyer: Ruth Law and Her Flying Machine* was my own fear of flying and my admiration for those early aviators who risked their lives. When I read about Ruth Law and her record-breaking cross-country flight from Chicago to New York City, I couldn't imagine the courage it took to fly in a flimsy flying machine made from bamboo and cloth. And what about the huge obstacles Ruth faced as a woman in 1916? Her persistence was remarkable.

But how could I write about Ruth without knowing what it was like to fly in an open cockpit? Since I couldn't find an early biplane, I decided to try paragliding. Up in the air, after

my heart stopped racing, a different feeling overcame me: exhilaration and freedom. I was flying . . . gliding . . . swooping . . . with amazing open views in every direction.

In that moment, I felt so connected to Ruth. I understood what she meant when she said, "The higher I soar, the greater freedom and liberty I feel." This inspired me to weave the theme of freedom into the story—the freedom Ruth felt as a pilot and sought as a woman.

My journey writing *Swimming with Sharks: The Daring Discoveries of Eugenie Clark* literally transformed me. I had been terrified of sharks and afraid to swim in the ocean ever since I saw the movie *Jaws* as a child.

Genie's close relationship with sharks fascinated me. Through my conversations with her, I discovered her profound curiosity and passion for them. This sense of wonder became a primary theme in the book.

When we met, Genie couldn't stop talking about an upcoming research trip and how she hoped to scuba dive—at the age of ninety-one! It was then that I knew I needed to experience her underwater world to successfully write about it, so I got certified to scuba dive.

By the time I plunged into the ocean, I had already learned from Genie the truth about sharks: "Sharks are magnificent and misunderstood." And when I saw my first shark underwater, I found myself following it.

My research journey not only informed my writing and the themes in the book, but also transformed my fear into a passion for sharks and reminded me to never judge based on rumors or appearance.

My book *Anybody's Game: Kathryn Johnston, the First Girl to Play Little League Baseball*, grew from my childhood passion: baseball. As a young girl, I rarely left the house without my mitt and ball, and I played catch every day with my father and brother.

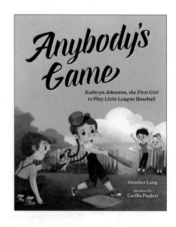

When my own kids started playing Little League, those special memories came flooding back. I had the urge to learn more about the history of women in baseball.

I was shocked to read about Kathryn's struggle to play Little League in 1950. I had no idea girls were prohibited from playing Little League baseball until 1974. I couldn't imagine what my childhood would have been like without baseball and softball. I knew I had to tell Kathryn's story.

Reading, researching, and writing nonfiction helps me grow in so many important ways. It's a chance to explore personal thinking, connect with our natural world, understand how people in the past have made things better for us today, find role models, overcome fears, and discover new passions. I hope the stories I share will inspire young readers to dream big and embrace their own journeys.

◎ April Pulley Sayre

April Pulley Sayre is a photo-illustrator and award-winning author of more than sixty-five books, including *Warbler Wave, Best in Snow, The Slowest Book Ever,* and *Thank You, Earth.* Her read-aloud picture books are known for their lyricism and scientific precision. *Raindrops Roll* was an ALA Notable and an Orbis Pictus Honor Book. *Eat Like a Bear* and *Rah, Rah, Radishes!* are among her other ALA Notables.

Nonfiction Mentor Texts

Grades 4–5; PB; STEM

Sayre, April Pulley. *Bloom Boom!* San Diego: Beach Lane/Simon & Schuster, 2019.

———. *Did You Burp? How to Ask Questions (or Not).* Watertown, MA: Charlesbridge, 2019.

———. *Like a Lizard.* Honesdale, PA: Boyds Mills, 2019.

———. *Raindrops Roll.* San Diego: Beach Lane/Simon & Schuster, 2015.

———. *Thank You, Earth: A Love Letter to Our Planet.* New York: Greenwillow, 2018.

Sharing Wonder and the Layers Beneath

My goal in life is to share wonder.

My daily life is steeped in mud and toads and wildflowers and adventures in rain forests. So I guess when you ask about how writing and illustrating nonfiction is personal, I think: How could writing and illustrating nonfiction *not* be personal?

Nonfiction authors are telling you about their love of the real world. They are exploring the home we live in, the sunsets that make our hearts swell, the plants that supply our food, the government and history that can cradle or crush our children's future and dreams. Nonfiction celebrates the life that supports us, from smiles to cells.

Of course, a story, a narrative, can spark connection. But so can a photo, a fact, a thought, an idea. These nonnarrative forms can inspire curiosity and help us understand where we are on the map of the world.

Connection is the basis of wonder. It's not just a childhood thing; it's what keeps us going even in hard times in life. Even grown-ups crave that puddle-jumping joy, that stop-and-stare curiosity, that spellbound sense that we are part of a larger picture.

Perhaps it appears that my 2019 books are about flowers, lizards, and questions. But here I'll let slip the secret keywords—their hidden book vibes:

Bloom Boom! = Exuberance. Kick-starting joy.

Like a Lizard = Goofy imitation. Surprise. Delight.

Did You Burp? How to Ask Questions (or Not) = Uh-oh mistakes. Trial and error. Empowerment. Inquiry.

Yes, what makes nonfiction live and breathe is voice and emotion. *Bloom Boom!* is a long-lasting bouquet of flowers. Perhaps someone will give it for Valentine's Day or some other holiday. It is a happy book, a simple read-aloud celebrating the colorful unfolding of mass blooms in the wild and in gardens. It has unseen roots, as flowers do.

There are places I danced with author friends among roads surrounded by bluebells. There are pathways I climb yearly with love for the returning trillium bloom. Yet the book also has images taken on road trips when my family was propelling itself through grueling grief, as well as photos I took while struggling to strengthen after a surgery.

Some photos make me long for my mom and grandma, who loved and showed me the flowers of the world. Yes, there is emotion flowing through the craft of nonfiction. Just watch me try to read *Thank You, Earth* without getting teary and you'll know that for sure.

For readers, though, I want these books to fly without me hovering over them and dictating what they should think or feel. I always wonder about the songwriter problem. You know: When you love a song, and it means something to you on a deep level. But then you hear the songwriter talk about it, and it means something different to them, and it kind of messes up what that song has become in your life and heart.

My editor, art director, and I pour ourselves into crafting a book that can sing on its own, without us. We want the reader to have an experience. That means taking some of the ego out of the book and allowing the words to suggest, not preach or overexplain. Nonetheless, intuitive readers will discover—in the word choice, the rhythm, the way the words flow—exactly how I feel.

When I submitted *Raindrops Roll*, I felt like my soul was trying to push itself out of my chest. At that time, this kind of book was new for me—and sort of nuts and experimental. I had just spent a summer dripping wet, photographing obsessively, and letting this whole foolish idea unfold. The book was joy—my wonder world, as a child, and today.

I was scared that my editor would not love it, that she would not see that this was the world to me. Thankfully, she did.

I hope my books will send readers back to the real world with refreshed eyes. That is the power of nonfiction.

Simply share wonder. That is what I hope to do.

⊚ Baptiste Paul

Baptiste Paul is a Caribbean-born author of three books for children. His debut picture book, *The Field*, received starred reviews from *Kirkus, The Horn Book*, and *Booklist*. According to *Kirkus*, his coauthored book *Adventures to School* "will pique readers' curiosity." His picture book biography, *I Am Farmer*, chronicles the work of Cameroonian environmentalist Tantoh Nforba. Learn more about Baptiste at baptistepaul.net.

Nonfiction Mentor Texts

Grades 4–6; PB; Bio/SS, SS

Paul, Baptiste, and Miranda Paul. *Adventures to School: Real-Life Journeys of Students from around the World. New York: Little Bee, 2018.*

———. *I Am Farmer: Growing an Environmental Movement in Cameroon.* Minneapolis, MN: Millbrook, 2019.

Digging Tunnels: A Story within a Story

Every story starts somewhere. Mine started before I was born.

How is this possible? I'll tell you a story.

When I started school, my mother held my hand all the way there. After each school day, she sat on a rocking chair and watched me do my schoolwork. Sometimes she would flip through my notebook and ask me to redo certain sections, citing where I did not give my best effort.

It would take me until high school to find out why she cared about my education so much.

I discovered that my mom was illiterate.

For years she had checked over pages and pages of work she couldn't even read. Her tunnel vision was focused on my education, even though she'd never enrolled in school herself.

I learned that my mother had been born into a system called indentured servitude. Instead of allowing her to go to school, her family prodded her into providing for the family by cleaning homes.

One day she stood on a chair, washing windows at a wealthy family's home. A boy and a girl around her age stepped out of the house, dressed in uniforms and carrying backpacks.

Later that evening, she asked if she could go to school. My grandmother's response was short and swift: "No."

For weeks she watched kids her age go to school. She wondered what it would be like to sit in a classroom. She wondered whether anyone would notice if she snuck away. So one day, she dropped her broom and journeyed one mile to the schoolhouse, barefoot.

To her surprise, the teacher welcomed her. She felt like she belonged, for one whole hour, until my grandmother stormed into the classroom and sent her back to work.

When my mom grew up, she ensured that all ten of her children went to school. Times were tough, our basic needs were never fully met, but every year she found a way to buy us each one pair of black rubber shoes. These shoes usually fell apart within a month, so I used glue, ropes, and vines to hand-stitch them back together. But eventually they were beyond repair. Then I would journey barefoot up the mountain to school, scraping tar and rocks off my feet.

When I was writing *Adventures to School: Real-Life Journeys of Students from around the World,* my experiences connected me to the children in the book in ways I didn't expect. Despite the hardships I overcame, my childhood adventures weren't dull or sad, and neither were the majority of these kids' experiences. I wanted to make sure that the children's stories were portrayed with honesty and that they captured both the difficulty and the joy. I wanted to make sure the dignity of each kid was preserved. My perspective led me to dig deeper to portray the information more richly and accurately than an outsider would.

Likewise, when I wrote *I Am Farmer: Growing an Environmental Movement in Cameroon*, I was telling the story of an amazing human who saves lives in his part of Africa—an ocean away from where I grew up and live now. But along the way, I drew on my own shared experiences. I remembered what it felt like to carry buckets of water on my head and to taste the breadfruit that I propagated. That plant still feeds my family, just as Farmer's banana trees do.

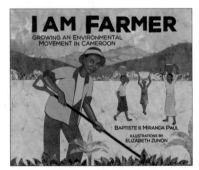

Some nonfiction writers gather information by mining historical archives and books and internet databases. For me, the juiciest details and rawest emotional connections come from mining my own experiences and listening to the people connected to the actual stories. Some people dislike nonfiction books being referred to as "stories," but that's what they are—stories that happen to be true.

If I can dig deep enough to look that story right in the eye, I might find a tunnel that connects cultures or leads to a brighter tomorrow. Just as my mom reached out her hand and guided me to school, I hope my books help to lead children into a world of new experiences.

Seth Fishman

Seth Fishman is a native of Midland, Texas, and a graduate of Princeton University and the University of East Anglia in Norwich, England. He is the author of the Mathical Book Prize winner and Boston Globe–Horn Book Honor nonfiction picture book *A Hundred Billion Trillion Stars*, along with *Power Up* and *The Ocean in Your Bathtub*. He runs the LA office of the Gernert Company, a literary agency, and lives with his wife and sons.

Nonfiction Mentor Text

Grades 4–6; PB; STEM

Fishman, Seth. *A Hundred Billion Trillion Stars.* New York: Greenwillow, 2017.

On Not Knowing, and the Beauty of Very, Very Big Things

My dad didn't know how to do anything.

Except, perhaps, read books, tell jokes, and find oil (he was a geologist in Texas). But I never learned any of the basic cool parenting things that both moms and dads often teach their kids, like how to fish, how to change the oil or a flat tire, how to camp, anything about gardening or lawn maintenance, woodworking (or, rather, how to handle dangerous tools), how to cook, or how to build or install furniture.

Before my son was born, I had something of a panic attack realizing that I had none of these bright and shiny stereotypical parental abilities. I even enrolled, with a friend, in a plumbing (very helpful!) and electrical wiring (helpful at teaching me not to do electrical wiring) course to learn useful around-the-house skills to fill in some of the gaps in my dad knowledge.

I played soccer a little, and ultimate Frisbee. I have an MFA in creative writing (the most useful degree). I like to read. I know I have something to offer, but what I really wanted was to be competent in all things, no matter how silly that sounds.

Since I couldn't do much handiwork, I decided that I would endeavor to answer all the questions my son would inevitably ask me.

Of course, I recognized that the key wasn't knowing answers; it was learning answers to his questions *together* in a way that's honest, interesting, and hopefully long-lasting. But back then, I remember thinking: What if he asks me how many stars there are in the sky and I don't know? He'll think me a failure. I know that's dramatic, but for a split second, it was true.

When I did the research and discovered the beautiful true number of stars—a hundred billion trillion—a picture book concept was born. The words and illustrations transition from the vast universe to the one person who mattered, my son. The book would do more than just list fun facts and big numbers. It would ignite a sense of wonder about things we don't understand and convey the idea that it's okay to not know. It would show that we all have a role to play, that we are a functional, important part of the vastness.

If I can help my son and other young readers gain a small moment of self-realization and universe-understanding, I'll feel that the book's purpose is fulfilled. And maybe my father taught me everything I needed to know after all.

@ Stephen R. Swinburne

Stephen R. Swinburne has worked as a national park ranger and is the author of more than thirty children's books. Travels to faraway lands such as Africa, Borneo, and Bangladesh, along with treks through Yellowstone and researching giraffes, have all influenced his book projects, including *Sea Turtle Scientist*; *Run, Sea Turtle, Run*; and *Giraffe Math*. Steve visits nearly a hundred schools a year across the United States as well as many international schools. He lives in Vermont with his wife, Heather. Find him at www.steveswinburne.com.

Nonfiction Mentor Texts

Grades 4–5, 5–8; PB, LF; STEM

Swinburne, Stephen R. *Run, Sea Turtle, Run: A Hatchling's Journey.* Minneapolis, MN: Millbrook, 2020. (Grades 4–6)

———. *Sea Turtle Scientist.* Boston, MA: Houghton Mifflin Harcourt, 2014. (Grades 5–8)

———. *Turtle Tide: The Ways of Sea Turtles.* Honesdale, PA: Boyds Mills, 2005. (Grades 4–6)

Inspired by Nature: Near and Far

I could not imagine writing a nonfiction piece that I didn't have an emotional connection with. Life experiences, past jobs, memories from my travels, books I've read, people I've met . . . all inform my nonfiction writing.

The morning I sat down to write about how sea turtles are incredible survivors, memories of being a National Park Service ranger on Cumberland Island National Seashore in Georgia came flooding back to me.

My official title was Backcountry Wilderness Ranger. My job was twofold: help campers in the island's backcountry and monitor Cumberland's incredible wildlife. I spent hours along Cumberland's seventeen-mile stretch of wild beach. I'll always remember my first encounter with a sea turtle.

As I walked close to the water line one warm, summer twilight, I noticed the distinctive tracks of a loggerhead turtle. I knew that only one set of tracks coming out of the surf meant the female turtle was still at the high tide line and had not returned to the sea. I crept up silently behind the nesting sea turtle and watched in awe as she tucked her precious bundle of Ping-Pong ball–sized eggs in a sandy hole. Little did I know that that first adventure with a wild sea turtle would lead to a lifelong fascination with and study of these creatures.

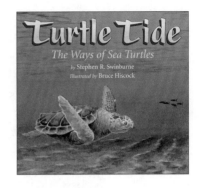

My Cumberland Island experience inspired my first children's book on sea turtles, *Turtle Tide: The Ways of Sea Turtles*. But as it turned out, I was not done writing about these incredible, endangered creatures.

I was thrilled when, a few years later, Houghton Mifflin Harcourt accepted my proposal for *Sea Turtle Scientist*, which became part of their Scientists in the Field series. I was intrigued by how scientists study an animal that spends 99 percent of its life at sea, far from the prying eyes of biologists.

While searching for a cover photograph of a leatherback sea turtle for *Sea Turtle Scientist*, I discovered the work of South American photographer Guillaume Feuillet. We used a few of Guillaume's photos in the book, but I thought about how cool it would be to showcase his photography in a book for very young children. With Guillaume's amazing pictures of leatherback hatchlings as inspiration, I wrote my third book about these remarkable marine reptiles, *Run, Sea Turtle, Run: A Hatchling's Journey*.

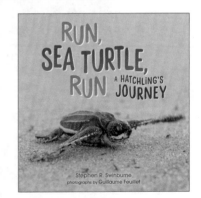

My passion for writing about wild creatures has led me to research animals far from home, including sea turtles in the Caribbean and giraffes in Africa. But ideas for writing are often found close to home, too, sometimes right under my nose. Watching monarch butterflies has inspired one of my latest projects. A patch of my neighbor's Vermont backyard has milkweed, and I've had the opportunity to follow the monarch life cycle from egg and larva to chrysalis and adult.

Researching monarchs led me to discover that this beautiful insect may be headed toward the endangered species list. Widespread use of herbicides in fields and pastures and along roadsides has destroyed millions of acres of monarch habitat.

Monarch Watch, an education-research-conservation organization, hopes to turn the tide of monarch habitat loss by restoring milkweed across the country. When I learned that their new Monarch Waystation Program encourages people to grow milkweed and nectar plants on their properties, I rototilled part of my backyard to create a monarch waystation. I've planted a few different kinds of milkweed and quite a few nectar plants, including cosmos, butterfly bush, and Mexican sunflower.

It's just a start, but I know, one day, monarch butterflies will have another place to raise their young and feed on flower nectar—a new home for butterflies. And perhaps a new book for me.

 Deborah Heiligman

Deborah Heiligman has always loved to research and write nonfiction, from the time she was a child to her first job at Scholastic Magazines and through her many years as a book author. For her, the old adage "write what you know" should be changed to "write what you don't know." There is nothing more exciting to Deborah than researching a new topic and then writing about it with her whole heart, soul, and mind. Visit her at www.DeborahHeiligman.com.

Nonfiction Mentor Texts

Grades 4–5, 5–8, 7–8; PB, LF; Bio/SS, Bio/STEM, STEM

Heiligman, Deborah. *The Boy Who Loved Math: The Improbable Life of Paul Erdös.* New York: Roaring Brook, 2013. (Grades 4–5)

———. *Charles and Emma: The Darwins' Leap of Faith.* New York: Square Fish, 2011. (Grades 5–8)

———. *From Caterpillar to Butterfly.* New York: HarperCollins, 1996. (Grades 4–5)

———. *Vincent and Theo: The van Gogh Brothers.* New York: Holt, 2017. (Grades 7–8)

Only Connect

The famous journalist Tom Wolfe said that every writer has a word or a phrase that is that writer's theme. Wolfe's was, not surprisingly, "status."

About ten years ago, my husband heard him say this at a talk, and asked me whether I knew my theme. I didn't have to think about it; I answered immediately: "Only connect." It's the epigraph to the E. M. Forster novel *Howard's End.*

For me, life is all about connecting to other people. When I look back at my books—my "books from the heart" and books on assignment, or projects too good to turn down—I realize that I always write about connection.

Sometimes I write about connections between people and animals (so far most notably in three fiction picture books I've written about my golden retriever, Tinka) or between people and plants (a middle grade biography about Barbara McClintock published almost twenty years ago and a current picture book project about her). *The Boy Who Loved Math: The Improbable Life of Paul Erdös* is about the connection of a boy with numbers. His connection with numbers led him to connect with people.

But usually I write about connections between people. In two of my YA non-fiction books, that connection is right in the title: *Charles and Emma: The Darwins' Leap of Faith* and *Vincent and Theo: The van Gogh Brothers*. It was the process of researching and writing the books that gave me a deep understanding of the connection between those pairs.

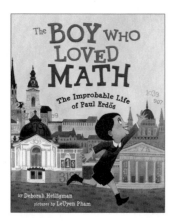 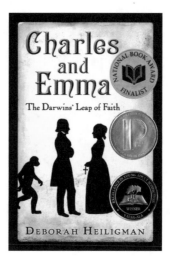 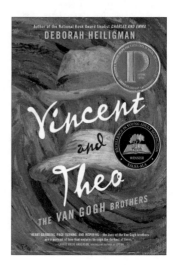

Why is "only connect" my theme? I'm a people person through and through. I got that from my mother, through both nature and nurture. Her favorite activity was people-watching.

From the time I was very young, I'd sit next to my mother—in a restaurant, in a hotel lobby, on a beach—and people-watch. She'd point out someone to me, discreetly, and we'd try to figure out that person's story. We'd suggest names and nationalities to each other, wondering about everything about them. My mother had a curiosity about everyone, a curiosity born from love for people—and story.

My mother had a lot of friends, and she made friends with strangers, getting to know them and their stories. I watched—and learned.

I didn't know it at the time, but that was the beginning of my life as a writer.

My mother died when I was just thirty-four. A few days

later, a neighbor I didn't know ran across the street to tell me about my mother, how much she would miss her. She said, smiling, tears running down her face, "I always felt *seen* by her." Yes. That was my mother.

As fate would have it, I had to write a book, on deadline, right after my mother died. That book, *From Caterpillar to Butterfly*, was reminiscent of the very first book I checked out of my elementary school library, *What Is a Butterfly?*

I had a vivid memory of my mother reading that book to me on my childhood bed. And so I researched and wrote, grieving. I told the story of a classroom of children, based on my son's preschool class, watching a caterpillar turn into a butterfly. But I was really writing about my mother, her life and her death. That book is about my connection to her and my letting her go. I'm sure nobody realizes it, but it is.

My father died five years after my mom. Cleaning out the house, I found multiple copies of *Writer's Digest*, with notes in my mother's handwriting. What? I asked her best friend, who told me, "Oh yes, your mother always wanted to be a writer." My mother never told me that, not even after I had published my first book. I guess she wanted me to have my own dream, not hers.

But my mother is the one who gave me that dream, I now realize. Her death, just as I was coming into my own as an adult, affected me greatly. I don't think I'll ever get over it. I think that's another reason I love writing about connections. My primary connection was terminated before I was ready, and I think I try to make up for that every day, with how I love and what I write.

 Candace Fleming

Candace Fleming is the author of more than forty books for children. Among her nonfiction titles are *The Family Romanov*, *Giant Squid*, and *The Rise and Fall of Charles Lindbergh*. She is the recipient of the *Los Angeles Times* Book Prize and the Orbis Pictus Award, as well as a two-time recipient of the Boston Globe–Horn Book Award. She is also a two-time recipient of the Sibert Honor, the YALSA Nonfiction Award, and the Golden Kite Award.

Nonfiction Mentor Texts

Grades 4–6, 5–8; PB, LF; Bio/SS, STEM

Fleming, Candace. *Amelia Lost: The Life and Disappearance of Amelia Earhart.* New York: Penguin Random House/Schwartz & Wade, 2011. (Grades 5–8)

———. *The Family Romanov: Murder, Rebellion, and the Fall of Imperial Russia.* New York: Penguin Random House/Schwartz & Wade, 2014. (Grades 5–8)

———. *Giant Squid.* New York: Roaring Brook, 2016. (Grades 4–6)

———. *The Great and Only Barnum: The Tremendous, Stupendous Life of Showman P. T. Barnum.* New York: Penguin Random House/Schwartz & Wade, 2009. (Grades 5–8)

———. *Honeybee: The Busy Life of Apis mellifera.* New York: Holiday House/Neal Porter Books, 2020. (Grades 4–6)

———. *The Lincolns: A Scrapbook Look at Abraham and Mary.* New York: Penguin Random House/Schwartz & Wade, 2008. (Grades 5–8)

Telling True Stories with My Whole Self

A few years ago, while teaching a class in nonfiction writing, a student confessed she'd chosen to write true stories because it was easier. Somewhere she'd gotten the impression that nonfiction is a lesser form of literature, that it doesn't require imagination or digging deep. She didn't recognize that the best nonfiction represents some larger meaning—pain or betrayal, love, faith, or hate, and that its writers do far more than string together a collection of facts.

Yes, I write nonfiction. But I am a storyteller, not a fact teller. And the true tales I write spring directly from my experiences, passions, heartbreaks, obsessions, fears, quirks, curiosities, beliefs, desires. Writing nonfiction is like sitting before a blank screen and scraping off a piece of myself. I'm always sure that after reading, say, *The Family Romanov* or *The Great and Only Barnum* people can see beneath my skin, that they will uncover as much about me as they will about my subjects. Let me explain further by telling you a story—a true one, of course.

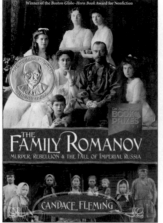

On July 3, 1937, my mother—thirteen years old at the time—was listening to *Fibber McGee and Molly* on the radio when an announcer broke in with stunning news: famous pilot Amelia Earhart was missing. En route to Howland Island on the last leg of her around-the-world flight, the aviator had simply vanished. Authorities believed she'd gone down at sea.

My mother couldn't believe it. It seemed impossible. To her, Amelia Earhart was the woman who could do anything—a larger-than-life role model who symbolized endless female possibilities. She couldn't be lost at sea. She just couldn't!

And so my mother stumbled out to her backyard and gazed up into the summer-blue sky. Watching . . . waiting . . . willing Amelia home. She was convinced that if she stood there long enough, she would eventually spy the pilot winging her way to safety.

But Amelia never came.

And she never came.

And despite the passing decades, whenever she told this story I could still hear the sadness and longing in her voice. Amelia Earhart had broken my mother's heart. And in turn, through my mother's memories, she'd broken mine.

Is it any wonder, then, that I embarked on a deeply researched, intimate exploration of Amelia Earhart's life? *Amelia Lost* is my search for the missing flyer, my attempt to return her to our world, my hope of mending broken hearts.

Here's another true story: Growing up in Central Illinois, I often played in the log cabin that Abraham Lincoln built for his parents. Weed-choked and forgotten, the place enchanted me. I'd climb up into its dusty loft, crawl down into its spidery root cellar, and pretend I was a settler on the prairie frontier. Sometimes I'd bicycle out to the local fairground, one of the Lincoln-Douglas debate sites, or flop onto the carpet-thick grass of the county courthouse where Abe once practiced law.

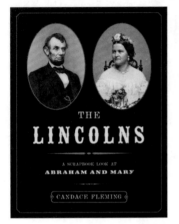

Most Fridays I slept over at my friend Emily's house. Back in 1856, Lincoln had slept a few nights there, too, and so we were forever pulling out the Ouija board. But no matter how hard we tried, we never managed to contact him. It didn't matter, though. I could hear him anyway. His voice seemed to echo from every street corner. Abraham Lincoln was always present, always there.

Decades later, when I wrote *The Lincolns*, I wasn't writing about an iconic American. I was writing about my childhood friend. I was writing about someone who was already deep in my bones. I was writing a part of me.

That's how it always works.

The Family Romanov? I was feeding a forty-year obsession with Russian history.

Giant Squid? I was satisfying my own curiosity.

Honeybee? All worker bees are female, and I'm a sucker for girl-empowerment stories.

Yes, my nonfiction stories are steeped in fact. But they are also told with due reverence, even if the subject itself is irreverent. They stand in for a larger message, each story a marker in our collective journey. They are recounted with accuracy and understanding, with context, and with an unwavering devotion to truth. But most particularly, they are told with my whole self. That sort of telling is never easy.

 Cynthia Levinson

Cynthia Levinson writes nonfiction for readers ages six and up. Her books have won the Golden Kite and Crystal Kite Awards, the Jane Addams Children's Book Award, the Social Justice Literature Award, and the Carter G. Woodson Book Award, among others. Previously, she taught prekindergarten through graduate students and worked in education policy. She and her coauthor husband live in Austin and Boston. Please contact her if you know how to use a steam oven.

Nonfiction Mentor Texts

Grades 4–6, 5–8, 6–8; PB, LF; Bio/SS, SS

Levinson, Cynthia. *Hillary Rodham Clinton: Do All the Good You Can.* New York: Harper-Collins/Balzer + Bray, 2016. (Grades 5–8)

———. *Watch Out for Flying Kids! How Two Circuses, Two Countries, and Nine Kids Confront Conflict and Build Community.* Atlanta, GA: Peachtree, 2015. (Grades 5–8)

———. *We've Got a Job: The 1963 Birmingham Children's March.* Atlanta, GA: Peachtree, 2012. (Grades 5–8)

———. *The Youngest Marcher: The Story of Audrey Faye Hendricks, a Young Civil Rights Activist.* New York: Simon & Schuster/Atheneum, 2017. (Grades 4–6)

Levinson, Cynthia, and Sanford Levinson. *Fault Lines in the Constitution: The Framers, Their Fights, and the Flaws That Affect Us Today.* Atlanta, GA: Peachtree, 2019. (Grades 6–8)

The Crazy Privilege of Writing Nonfiction for Kids

"Cynthia Levinson did an insane amount of research!"

That's what a librarian said after reading *Watch Out for Flying Kids! How Two Circuses, Two Countries, and Nine Kids Confront Conflict and Build Community.* She had a good point. Here's a small sample of my insanity:

- 3 trips to Israel

- 2 trips to St. Louis

- 1 trip each to Sarasota, Chicago, and Saratoga Springs, New York

- 1 Hebrew translator and 2 Arabic translators

- Multiple in-depth interviews with 9 teenage circus performers in 3 languages and dozens of other people via Skype, Facebook, email, IM, telephone, and in person
- Books in my bibliography on politics in the Middle East and Midwest, the circus since Roman times, and equilibristics
- Lessons in juggling, wire-walking, globe-walking, silks, trapeze, and lyra (I was not crazy enough to unicycle.)

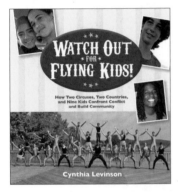

Why would anyone spend three years doing this and more—much more—to write a book for ten- to fourteen-year-olds?

Although there were times when I thought the research itself would drive me crazy (understandably, teenagers don't consider confiding in a sixty-five-plus-year-old writer a high priority), the reason was not in my head but in my heart: I cared deeply about these teens. Through "social circus" programs that bring together kids who would never otherwise meet or get along, they've overcome cultural, linguistic, and physical barriers as daunting as high buildings and reached literally soaring accomplishments.

In St. Louis's Circus Harmony, these kids include:

- Kellin, a juggler, home-schooled by his mother, Jessica, Circus Harmony's founder
- Iking, a street tumbler and gang member

In Israel's Galilee Circus, they include:

- Hla, an observant Muslim contortionist afraid of Jews
- Roey, a Jewish diabolo juggler, afraid of just about everything, including bugs

Practicing, performing, and traveling together, all of these kids became unlikely friends and stars. They have much to teach us, and I *had* to tell their stories, regardless of the time and cost.

My debut middle grade nonfiction book, *We've Got a Job: The 1963 Birmingham Children's March*, and a successor, the picture book biography *The Youngest Marcher: The Story of Audrey Faye Hendricks, a Young Civil Rights Activist*, similarly propelled me. These books focus on four of the three to four thousand children who protested segregation and went to jail, some for a week. Audrey was only nine.

They overcame their barriers while I attended a segregated high school, only dimly and distantly aware of their sacrifices and courage. Four years; multiple trips; dozens of books, articles, and documents; and countless interviews went into these two books. But compared to their efforts, mine seem minimal.

Although my editor didn't realize it when she asked me to write a biography of a presidential candidate, *Hillary Rodham Clinton: Do All the Good You Can* has a personal connection also. We were college dormmates!

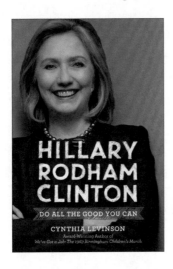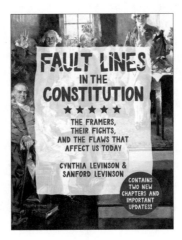

Fault Lines in the Constitution: The Framers, Their Fights, and the Flaws That Affect Us Today is personal for a different reason. I wrote it with my husband, a law professor. It's his life work translated into kid-speak, and our daughters and their husbands—two lawyers, an epidemiologist, and an education professor—all contributed vital information.

Writing nonfiction for young readers is a privilege that allows authors to pursue and share our curiosities, passions, concerns, and values.

⊚ Laurie Ann Thompson

Laurie Ann Thompson writes for young people to help them understand the world we live in so they can make it a better place for all, as seen in her award-winning nonfiction books, including *Emmanuel's Dream*, a picture book biography of Emmanuel Ofosu Yeboah, which was the recipient of the Schneider Family Book Award and named an ALA Notable Book and a CCBC Choice, among other accolades. She lives outside Seattle with her family. Learn more at lauriethompson.com.

Nonfiction Mentor Texts

Grades 4–6, 5–8, 7–8; PB, LF; Bio/SS, How-to, STEM/SS

Thompson, Laurie Ann. *Be a Changemaker: How to Start Something That Matters.* New York: Simon Pulse/Beyond Words, 2014. (Grades 7–8)

———. *Emmanuel's Dream: The True Story of Emmanuel Ofosu Yeboah.* New York: Penguin Random House/Schwartz & Wade, 2015. (Grades 4–6)

Paquette, Ammi-Joan, and Laurie Ann Thompson. *Two Truths and a Lie: Forces of Nature.* New York: Walden Pond Press, 2019. (Grades 5–8)

———. *Two Truths and a Lie: Histories & Mysteries.* New York: Walden Pond Press, 2019. (Grades 5–8)

———. *Two Truths and a Lie: It's Alive!* New York: Walden Pond Press, 2018. (Grades 5–8)

Finding My Why

I've always enjoyed reading nonfiction. Some of my favorite childhood memories are of lazy afternoons spent sprawled on the floor in front of my family's encyclopedia set, letting fate decide which random topic I would learn about next. So perhaps it seems only natural that I would be drawn to writing nonfiction, too.

But there was another, secret, reason for my choice. As a beginning writer, I thought writing nonfiction would be safer. I knew that writing good fiction requires the author to be vulnerable, to bare a part of their soul. Sharing our imaginations with readers, after all, invites them to take a peek at the inner workings of our minds—and judge us for it! Terrifying, right?

I wasn't nearly so bold, and I thought nonfiction would be the easy way out. Nonfiction is just facts, right? Boy, did I have a lot to learn!

For years I worked on draft after draft of the manuscript that eventually became *Emmanuel's Dream*, a true story about an inspiring man from Ghana who was born with a deformed leg. I'd done the research and written a competent biography, but I kept getting feedback that there was "something missing."

At one point, my well-meaning and incredibly supportive husband said something along the lines of, "Why are you [an able-bodied white woman from Wisconsin] writing this story anyway?" Ouch. He had a point. What *did* I have in common with Emmanuel? Why was I writing this story in the first place?

It turns out those were exactly the questions I needed to ask. I had all the facts lined up in a satisfying order, but what was missing was . . . *me*.

I'd been so focused on the facts that I'd left out my feelings. But isn't authentic human emotion just another kind of truth? And isn't it, perhaps, the most important truth to share with others?

When I finally got clear about my "why" for telling the story, the "how" to best tell it revealed itself almost immediately. For me, it isn't a story about having a disability or even about Emmanuel himself. It's about being left out and overlooked, feeling frustrated by injustice and inequality, and wanting to make the world a better place.

Those are all things I felt deeply as a child, and things I still relate to as an adult. The book reveals as much about me, I think, as it does about Emmanuel. So much for nonfiction being the easy way out!

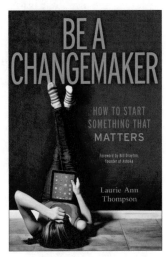

Since then, I've grown more comfortable sharing myself with readers, and I use this approach for every book I write. Curiosity about a subject isn't enough; I need to know *why* I'm curious about it.

In my teen how-to guide, *Be a Changemaker: How to Start Something That Matters*, for example, my "why" was the intense yearning to change the world that I had felt as a young person and the frustration and disappointment of not knowing how. That "why" helped me shape both the structure and the content of the book.

In my middle grade series, Two Truths and a Lie (coauthored with Ammi-Joan Paquette), my "why" is the joy of exploring encyclopedias and discovering new and surprising

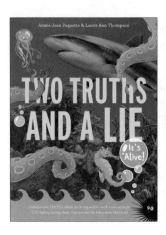 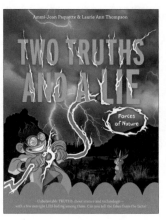 

things. I want readers to revel in their curiosity and delight in newfound knowledge, just like I do.

These days, the first question I ask myself when considering a new project is, "Why?" The answers help me choose which ideas to pursue and then guide me through the writing process from initial research to publication.

Writing books in this way allows readers to see who I really am while also learning about the topic at hand. And I've been surprised to realize that revealing myself to readers is one of the most rewarding aspects of being an author.

My favorite fan letters say things like: "It was the first time I ever saw myself in a book," and "Thank you for showing me it's okay to be like this," and "It feels like you wrote this just for me!"

What could possibly be better than that?

When I began my writing career, I never dreamed a nonfiction author could connect with readers on a deeply personal level. But don't we all write—and read, for that matter—to connect with other human beings? The best books establish that connection through both authenticity and vulnerability. So all authors, whether they're writing fiction or nonfiction, owe it to their readers to dig deep . . . terrifying or not.

⑨ Donna Janell Bowman

Donna Janell Bowman is the Texas author of many award-winning and celebrated nonfiction books for young readers. She is naturally drawn to underdog stories, buried histories, and other fascinating topics that keep her awake at night. A self-professed research addict, Donna has traveled across the country and around the world to ensure her books' accuracy. She has a Master of Fine Arts in Writing from Vermont College of Fine Arts and enjoys writing, coaching, and speaking to writers of all ages. She's online at www.donnajanellbowman.com.

Nonfiction Mentor Texts

Grades 4–8; PB; Bio/SS

Bowman, Donna Janell. *Abraham Lincoln's Dueling Words*. Atlanta, GA: Peachtree, 2018.

———. *Step Right Up: How Doc and Jim Key Taught the World about Kindness*. New York: Lee & Low, 2016.

My Heart Is in My Books

It is remarkable that each children's book writer is drawn to some ideas but not to others. What compels us to spend years of our lives distilling research into books for kids? How does a singular subject cast such a spell on us? Why nonfiction? Why us? Why me?

I'm especially intrigued by the challenges of writing narrative picture book biographies about people from the past. It took many years for me to realize that the answer to my *why* question goes deeper than the challenge of resurrecting a dead person on the page. And it all began in my childhood.

I grew up on a Quarter Horse ranch surrounded by a myriad of pets and farm animals, including a pet skunk. And horses. Did I mention the horses? I was a horse-crazy girl and a lucky beneficiary of the human-animal bond. But, far away from friends and family, I often felt isolated. Lonely. I became a writer in those wide-open spaces where curiosity and a vivid imagination blossomed.

People fascinated me. I became naturally nosy.

When my mother shared childhood stories about the rag man, the armory, or her Italian-speaking grandmother in the upstairs flat of her inner-city Chicago neighborhood, I was mesmerized. During rare trips to visit her family, I was a sponge for my grandmother's stories. Understanding my mother's background and her people helped me understand her.

But my father was a contradiction. To the rest of the world, he was a charming, funny, successful man. But at home, he was a closed book. He never spoke about his earlier life and never introduced us to his people. He died while I was in my twenties, taking with him all details about his WWII experiences, family lore, his own early quirks, hobbies, traumas, passions. I was left with unanswered questions about what made my complicated father tick. The omission felt like a void in my own identity.

It seems obvious now that my fascination with people is rooted in my attempt to understand my father, my people, myself.

The nonfiction story ideas that find me likewise tug at my heartstrings. Most often they begin with a simple curiosity—something I read, hear, watch, dream. I tend to be drawn to underdog stories and obscure bits of history that have been veiled by the dusty cobwebs of time.

The initial spark for *Step Right Up: How Doc and Jim Key Taught the World about Kindness* was the "educated" horse Beautiful Jim Key. But it was learn-

ing about the tenacious spirit of formerly enslaved William "Doc" Key, and the indelible impact he and Jim had on the emerging humane movement, that kept me motivated throughout the book's ten-year journey.

See, during my early years of horse shows and working for a veterinarian as a teenager, I witnessed many cases of animal abuse and bullying. The heartbreak and helplessness never left me. Perhaps sharing Doc and Jim's story was my way of speaking up. My heart is so embedded in the

story that I had my late father's stallion "sign" my publishing contract with his hoofprint. *Step Right Up* is a call to action to be kinder to animals and to each other. I'm there on every page.

For *Abraham Lincoln's Dueling Words*, the initial spark came from the shock of learning that Honest Abe, the man who wrote and choreographed some of the most powerful, inspiring, important words in our country's history, once wrote something so mean and offensive that he was challenged to a duel. (Spoiler alert: Lincoln survived!) Lincoln owed James Shields an apology.

My manuscript had already been acquired when I discovered where my heart connects to the story. First, it was the reminder that words have the power to inspire or to harm. And how we respond to our mistakes defines our character. Which brings me to an epiphany.

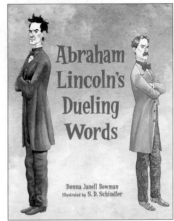

When *Step Right Up* was nearing print time, I was mulling over my dedication for that book while walking my dog. Then, *wham*! An inner voice interrupted my thoughts with a premature dedication for *Abraham Lincoln's Dueling Words*: *To my brother, because we owe each other an apology.*

Whoa! I had written an apology book without realizing it. I didn't ultimately use that dedication in the book, but it's whispering there between the lines.

Yes, my heart is woven into everything I write, even when I don't realize it. After researching the dickens out of my subjects, my inner storyteller frames a narrative through the lens of my own life experiences.

During every project, I learn a little more about myself, my people, and the human condition. I hope young readers will learn a bit more about themselves, too.

◎ Patricia Newman

Patricia Newman writes books that inspire young readers to seek connections to the real world. Her titles encourage readers to use their imaginations to solve real-world problems and act on behalf of their communities. The recipient of numerous awards, Patricia frequently speaks at schools and conferences to share how children of any age can affect change. Visit her at www.patriciamnewman.com.

Nonfiction Mentor Texts

Grades 4–8; LF; STEM

Newman, Patricia. *Eavesdropping on Elephants: How Listening Helps Conservation.* Minneapolis, MN: Millbrook, 2019.

———. *Sea Otter Heroes: The Predators That Saved an Ecosystem.* Minneapolis, MN: Millbrook, 2017.

———. *Zoo Scientists to the Rescue.* Minneapolis, MN: Millbrook, 2018.

Putting the Heart in Nonfiction

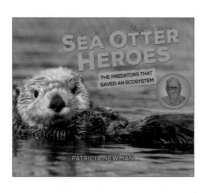

In my Sibert Honor acceptance speech for *Sea Otter Heroes*, I mentioned a teacher who once defined nonfiction as the facts and fiction as the heart. I'll be honest; she hurt my feelings.

My books—part biography, part science adventure—tell inspiring true stories of scientists who make a difference. Just as fiction authors write about themes that resonate with them, so too do nonfiction authors. My themes first have to light *my* fire with a personal connection, a narrative, and a Wow! factor. The Common Core State Standards might tempt readers to say my purpose is to "persuade, inform, or entertain." But my purpose goes way beyond that. I hope my stories empower children and show them their voices matter.

I wrote *Sea Otter Heroes* as a mystery to explore the idea that we don't know what we don't know. Marine biologist Brent Hughes connected the dots to discover that endangered sea otters are responsible for the health of a seagrass ecosystem. Seagrass sequesters carbon, provides a nursery for our food supply as it matures, and calms the waves that pound our coastlines. Without protection, sea otters and the benefits they provide could be lost to us and future generations. I want my readers to understand the effects of our actions.

I was raised to care for myself, my family, and my community. My husband calls me a professional volunteer. Building a performing arts center at my children's former high school is one example of my many projects. Time commitment: ten-plus years.

As a child, I spent a lot of time outside. I played kickball in the street, hiked, ice skated, built snow tunnels, rode my bike, fished, planted trees, and sailed on Malletts Bay (hello, fellow Vermonters!). I collected bugs and pressed fall leaves for my season-deprived friend in Florida. I even read outside. The outdoors was part of me.

Clearly, there's a connection between my love of the outdoors, my urge to volunteer, and the environmental books I write. But there's more to it. Like fiction, nonfiction comes from emotion. For me, that usually means feelings of injustice and confusion: Injustice over problems such as mountains of marine debris or elephant and rhino poaching. Confusion over how my time (and money) might be most effective.

My challenge is to simultaneously tell the truth, inspire, and offer hope for myself and my readers. In my books, hope is synonymous with science.

I used to volunteer for the San Diego Zoo, and I traveled to Kenya on a safari led by one of the zoo's geneticists. During the trip, I became fascinated by elephants' social relationships and cognitive capabilities. *Eavesdropping on*

Elephants explores the value of listening to them in order to save them from extinction. I added QR codes to the narrative to bring readers into the forest to see and hear the elephants as the scientists did. The closer we get to the wild, the more we care.

As a former zoo volunteer, I understand how zoos promote conservation, but many people don't. *Zoo Scientists to the Rescue* braids together three fascinating success stories about endangered species and the zoo scientists who protect them. These scientists go to incredible lengths to save orangutans, black-footed ferrets, and black rhinos, and they started out as children who loved animals. Readers identify with that. One mother wrote to say, "My son is now more than ever convinced that he wants to study animals. . . . [Y]ou lit a fire in him with this book. For that, I am grateful!"

Ultimately, my books meet an emotional need within me. But if my writing also resonates with readers, I know they've found the heart I've woven through the pages.

◎ Paula Yoo

Paula Yoo is a writer and musician. Her books range from the picture book biographies *Sixteen Years in Sixteen Seconds*, *Shining Star*, and *Twenty-Two Cents* to YA books, including *Good Enough* and *From a Whisper to a Rallying Cry: The Killing of Vincent Chin and the Trial That Galvanized the Asian American Movement*. As a screenwriter, she has sold TV pilots and written for shows such as NBC's *The West Wing* and The CW's *Supergirl*.

When she's not writing, Paula likes to play her violin. Visit her at https://paula yoo.com.

Nonfiction Mentor Texts

Grades 4–6, 7–8; PB, LF; Bio/Arts, Bio/SS, Bio/Sports

Yoo, Paula. *From a Whisper to a Rallying Cry: The Killing of Vincent Chin and the Trial That Galvanized the Asian American Movement*. New York: Norton Young Readers, 2021. (Grades 7–8)

———. *Shining Star: The Anna May Wong Story*. New York: Lee & Low, 2009. (Grades 4–6)

———. *Sixteen Years in Sixteen Seconds: The Sammy Lee Story*. New York: Lee & Low, 2005. (Grades 4–6)

———. *Twenty-Two Cents: Muhammad Yunus and the Village Bank*. New York: Lee & Low, 2014. (Grades 4–6)

Finding My New Voice

My first nonfiction children's book happened by accident. Or so I thought.

In 2002, I stumbled on an article about Dr. Sammy Lee. I learned he was the first Asian American man to win a gold medal in diving at the Olympics.

I had never heard of Sammy Lee before. The article fascinated me, and I fell into a rabbit hole as I devoured information about this world-renowned athlete.

As a Korean American, I was inspired by Sammy Lee's triumph over racism. I wished I had known about him when I was growing up. His positive story would have helped me cope better with the many painful incidents of racism I experienced as a child and a teenager.

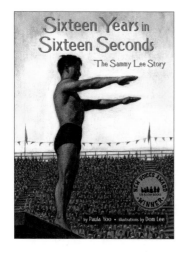

When I discovered that no children's book had ever been written about Sammy Lee, I decided to write *Sixteen Years in Sixteen Seconds: The Sammy Lee Story*.

An early reader advised me that my manuscript might not have a chance with mainstream publishers. After all, according to statistics compiled by the Cooperative Children's Book Center (CCBC), out of 3,150 children's books published in 2002, only 46 (1 percent) were written by Asian Pacifics/Asian Pacific Americans and only 91 (less than 3 percent) were about Asian Pacifics/Asian Pacific Americans.* (The statistics for other diverse groups were just as discouraging.)

I ended up submitting my manuscript to Lee & Low's annual New Voices contest for writers of color. To my shock, it won!

Lee & Low published *Sixteen Years in Sixteen Seconds* in 2005. That year, out of the 2,800 children's books published, 60 were written by Asian Pacific American authors and 64 books were about Asian subjects or characters. The statistics were still deplorable, but I was delighted that MY book was part of that 2 percent.

That inspired me to write more children's biographies of important Asian historical figures. I suddenly had a mission—to make sure our community was represented, to make sure our stories and our voices were heard.

This led to two more picture book biographies—*Shining Star: The Anna May Wong Story*, about Asian American film star Anna May Wong,

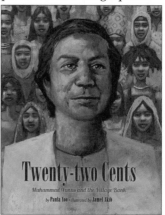

and *Twenty-Two Cents: Muhammad Yunus and the Village Bank*, about Nobel Peace Prize winner Muhammad Yunus.

CCBC statistics from 2019 show that out of 3,716 books published in the United States, 379 were written by Asian/Asian Americans and 334 were about Asian/Asian American people

---

*Data on books by and about people of color and from First/Native Nations published for children and teens compiled by the Cooperative Children's Book Center, School of Education, University of Wisconsin-Madison. See https://ccbc.education.wisc.edu/books/pcstats.asp.

or issues.** That's barely 10 percent of all books published. We still have a long way to go.

Statistics are just as grim in our educational system. The absence of Asian American and Pacific Islander history in our school curricula, along with the erasure of Asian Americans in the media and in Hollywood, has far-reaching and disturbing implications for how white people and other non-Asians view us. It leads not only to ignorance and racism, but also to the treatment of all Asians as the perpetual foreign "Other."

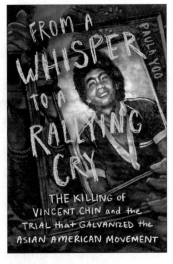

All of this drives my mission—and *passion*—to chronicle the important contributions Asian Americans and Pacific Islanders have made in our country. My YA book *From a Whisper to a Rallying Cry: The Killing of Vincent Chin and the Trial That Galvanized the Asian American Movement* also focuses on Asian American issues and history. It describes how the 1982 beating death of a Chinese American man by two white autoworkers in Detroit galvanized the Asian American civil rights movement.

As I look back on my writing career, I realize that my first nonfiction children's book did *not* happen by accident. It was fate. I will continue to write nonfiction in the hope that the struggles endured by Dr. Sammy Lee, Anna May Wong, Muhammad Yunus, and Vincent Chin will never happen again.

** See https://ccblogc.blogspot.com/2020/06/the-numbers-are-in-2019-ccbc-diversity.html?fbclid=IwAR 35Emvmeah5owiiAaD8ZFhy15Lihyn4zKK4ttetbllA87-X3makQ7r_OHU.

 Nancy F. Castaldo

Environmental educator Nancy F. Castaldo puts her science degree to work writing award-winning STEM books for kids. Her titles have appeared on countless booklists, received starred reviews, and earned awards, including the Green Earth Book Award. Nancy is a National Geographic Certified Educator. She strives to inform, inspire, and empower young readers with each book. When she isn't writing or researching, she's often hiking with her camera. Visit her at www.nancy castaldo.com.

Nonfiction Mentor Texts

Grades 4–8, 5–8, 7–8; LF; STEM

Castaldo, Nancy F. *Beastly Brains: Exploring How Animals Think, Talk, and Feel.* Boston: Houghton Mifflin Harcourt, 2017. (Grades 5–8)

————. *Sniffer Dogs: How Dogs (and Their Noses) Save the World.* Boston: Houghton Mifflin Harcourt, 2014. (Grades 4–8)

————. *The Story of Seeds: Our Food Is in Crisis. What Will You Do to Protect It?* Boston: Houghton Mifflin Harcourt, 2020. (Grades 7–8)

The Seeds of Childhood

I often show a photo during my school visits of me as a little girl holding something very special, a little nonfiction book about planting seeds called *What Shall I Put in the Hole That I Dig?* I loved that book so much that I still have it on my shelf. That little girl grew up to write *The Story of Seeds: Our Food Is in Crisis. What Will You Do to Protect It?* I really dug deep (sorry) into my childhood curiosity to write that one.

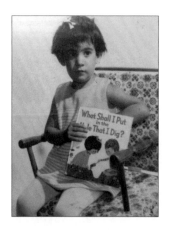

When I learned that seeds were going extinct, just like animals, it woke up that long-ago passion inside of me to learn more, like a dormant seed that was just waiting to germinate so many years later. In fact, I was surprised at my obsession with the topic.

I spent eight years, on and off, researching until the book was published. It was as if the idea for that book was just waiting to sprout until I grew up.

The subject of *Sniffer Dogs: How Dogs (and Their Noses)*

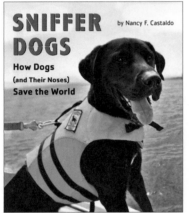

Save the World was not as much of a surprise to me. There was nothing dormant about it. Dogs and I go way back. As an only child, my dogs were like siblings, and the first job I ever wanted was to be a veterinarian. In my early pursuit of that dream, I took a pre-vet 4-H class and volunteered in a local animal shelter. I'd bathe and walk the dogs to socialize them for adoption.

I spent days with dogs, many of whom were rescues, during my *Sniffer Dogs* research. Hour after hour was spent getting to know them, photographing them, and sharing their stories. It was pure joy! And it wasn't just the dogs that made the process fun; the handlers were pretty awesome, too. Creating that book was the culmination of so many things I love—dogs, photography, science, and writing. My dog, Gatsby, was even included in the pages.

Every book means something special to an author-illustrator. We put a little of ourselves into each creation. *Beastly Brains: Exploring How Animals Think, Talk, and Feel* is also rooted in my childhood.

I was fortunate to have a curious mom who filled her bookshelves with titles about all sorts of nonfiction subjects. One of her favorites was dolphins. I don't know whether there were any books published about dolphins that we didn't have. I pored over those books and the family copies of *National Geographic*. As a middle school student, I used them for report research. As an adult children's book author, I went back to them to begin my research for *Beastly Brains*. I dedicated the book to my mom. She was the first person to make it clear to me that animals feel, think, and communicate.

We are all the products of our childhood. The books and media we are exposed to help shape us into the adults we will become. I am the daughter of parents who encouraged my curiosity. I was also influenced by books and movies, including *Bambi*, *Doctor Doolittle*, and *The Jungle Book*. The child in me who wanted to roam the jungle like Mowgli, talk to the animals like Doctor Doolittle, and protect animals like Bambi is in my head as I write. After all, I'm still writing for that nature-loving kid.

 Lee Wind

Lee Wind, superhero job: author of *No Way, They Were Gay? Hidden Lives and Secret Loves* and the YA novel, *Queer as a Five-Dollar Bill*, a *Publishers Weekly* "Indie Success Story." Lee's award-winning blog for LGBTQ+ youth is *I'm Here. I'm Queer. What the Hell Do I Read?* Lee's Clark Kent job: the director of marketing and programming at the Independent Book Publishers Association and the official blogger for SCBWI. Learn more at www.leewind.org.

Nonfiction Mentor Text

Grades 5–8; LF; Bio/SS

Wind, Lee. *No Way, They Were Gay? Hidden Lives and Secret Loves.* Minneapolis, MN: Zest Books/Lerner, 2021.

How Primary Sources Saved Me (and Might Just Save the World)

I grew up with a history deficiency.

Let me explain. I'm gay, and yet the way history was taught in schools, the way it was presented in books, nobody before me—at any time, or anywhere around the world—had ever been a guy who like-liked other guys.

I felt so alone. So ashamed of who I was and how I felt.

So I dated girls, judging it the right thing to do, but not *feeling* what I knew I was supposed to feel. I was bullied for not being "manly" enough. I forced my voice lower so no one would suspect. I hid my truth. Every minute of every day. And I hated myself.

By the time I finally came out in my twenties, I had discovered there were others like me, but as far as I knew, LGBTQ+ history stretched back only to the Stonewall Rebellion in 1969.

History beyond that didn't include me, so I didn't include it.

It was 2011 when I first heard about Abraham Lincoln's letters to Joshua Fry Speed, letters that convinced some people that Abraham had been in love with Joshua.

Abraham Lincoln

Joshua Fry Speed

I didn't see how that could be true, but I went to the library and checked out a book that contained the letters.

What I read blew my mind. After living with Abraham in Springfield, Illinois, for four years, Joshua moved back to Kentucky and married a woman named Fanny. Eight months later, on October 5, 1842, Abraham wrote him and asked:

> But I want to ask a closer question, "Are you now in feeling as well as in judgment, glad that you are married as you are?" From anybody but me this would be an impudent question, not to be tolerated, but I know you will pardon it in me. Please answer it quickly, as I feel impatient to know.*

We don't have Joshua's answer, but we do know it was only four weeks later that Abraham married Mary Todd.

In *judgment* but not in *feeling*.

It was exactly how I had felt, back when I dated girls. Suddenly, there I was in history! Abraham Lincoln was a guy who like-liked another guy, just like me!

Goose bumps.

It was history vitamins—history nourishment. And I needed it. I read everything I could find about Abraham and Joshua, especially their letters, and became more and more convinced. I longed for a time machine so I could go back to tell my eleven-year-old self the news: *You're not alone.*

---

*Kincaid, Robert L. *Joshua Fry Speed: Lincoln's Most Intimate Friend*. Harrogate, TN: Department of Lincolniana, Lincoln Memorial University, 1943, pp. 54–55.

That's when I realized I *had* to share my goose bump moment with young people. I want them to see themselves in history. And I want to empower them to be their authentic selves as soon as it's safe for them to do so. Hopefully, NOW.

Abraham and Joshua led me to more Queer history, stories *sometimes* shared with adults but mostly kept from children. I'm not an adventurer, but I felt like one discovering Mahatma Gandhi's soulmate—not his wife, Kasturba, but the German Jewish architect Hermann Kallenbach. I read about Eleanor Roosevelt's love affair with Lorena Hickok and learned how Sappho's poems about her love for other women changed the way our culture thinks about love today. I found out that 3,500 years ago, the Pharaoh Hatshepsut changed how they presented their gender while they ruled Egypt, and I watched video interviews from the 1980s with Christine Jorgensen, world famous for transitioning their body to match who they knew they were on the inside.

No Way, They Were Gay? Hidden Lives and Secret Loves shares all these stories and more. It puts the primary sources in front of young people and lets them discover men who loved men, women who loved women, and people who lived outside gender boundaries in history. It lets them find themselves, and their friends, and their classmates, in history.

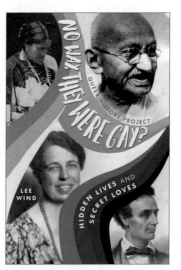

Knowing there were Queer people throughout history changes everything. It shows us that LGBTQ+ people deserve a place at the table today. And if we have a place at the table, it lets us—and everyone else—know that tomorrow, we can achieve anything!

LGBTQ+ history does one more thing: it helps dismantle the myth that the only important people of the past were rich, white, able-bodied men from Europe who were hetero and cisgendered. The truth is there were poor people, and people of color, and disabled people, and women, and people from all over the world, and men who loved men, and women who loved women, and people who lived outside gender boundaries. And they all made a difference in our world!

And knowing that empowers everyone.

So that's how I healed myself: by discovering my—*our*—Queer history. I really do believe it can change the world, one reader at a time.

Maybe even you.

Heather L. Montgomery

Heather L. Montgomery writes for kids who are wild about animals—the weirder, the wackier, the better. An award-winning science educator, Heather uses yuck appeal to engage young minds. She has published numerous nonfiction books, including *Something Rotten: A Fresh Look at Roadkill*; *Bugs Don't Hug: Six-Legged Parents and Their Kids*; and *Who Gives a Poop? Surprising Science from One End to the Other*. Inquiry is her life. Find her at www.HeatherLMontgomery.com.

Nonfiction Mentor Text

Grades 5–8; LF; STEM

Montgomery, Heather L. *Something Rotten: A Fresh Look at Roadkill*. New York: Bloomsbury, 2018.

A Compost of Questions

My passion is getting kids hooked on nature. For many years, I worked as an environmental educator. Leading kids knee-deep in a stream, paddling through a rock-walled canyon, standing under a rushing waterfall—that's how I connected students to nature. I've taught tens of thousands of kids.

I never considered becoming a writer until, one day, it hit me: I can physically teach only a certain number of kids. But if I write my ideas down, they can be shared across the globe. Words on a page carry into the future.

I'm also passionate about inquiry. Where did this passion come from? Recently when hiking deep in the Smokey Mountains with a friend, Kendra, and my brother, Fred, I got a clue about that.

Stopped in the middle of the trail under a grand tulip poplar tree, I mused, "I feel sorry for kids who don't get this."

Kendra looked puzzled.

"I don't mean the big trees—but that's a shame, too—I mean this," I waved my hand between my brother and myself. The whole hike we had been asking bizarre questions (What is in that millipede's poop? Why do those bat boxes have holes in their sides? What is that clear goop?). We made guesses and pointed out evidence. A friendly competition pervaded our conversation.

We've always done that. Inquiry is a part of my family culture. We'd never thought of it as an educational strategy or a scientific approach, but looking back, I see my life is rooted in a compost of questions. And that formed the foundation for the way I approached the hardest book topic I've ever tackled: roadkill.

For the longest time, I was scared of that topic. Every time I passed a carcass on the road, things inside my body wrenched. My heart screamed at the injustice, but my mind marveled at the bobcat's body. My eyes teared with sadness while my fingers begged to touch that velvet fur. And when I considered aloud possibly writing about roadkill, people looked at me like

Heather examining a wild boar.

I'd grown horns. But I couldn't stop myself from parking and looking, from asking and wondering. I felt like a voyeur, but my feet kept inching closer, closer to the dead bodies.

Then one day I gave into inquiry. It took over my life.

The next few years were a roller coaster of research. Depending on the day or even the moment, I felt angst that tore at my core, elation that soared like a hawk, or hope that suddenly surfaced like a mountain spring. That research was for me. No way could I consider writing about it for kids. But at that point, I didn't care; I *had* to know more.

The thing is, every sad body drew me into far flung topics—topics I'd never been that interested in, like math (studying the deaths of mama turtles, mean, meridian, and mode became relevant to me) and art history (thanks to an artist who recycles the skins of roadkill). That, I realized, is how it could be for my readers. What if this inquiry could get them hooked on nature? Suddenly, I *had* to write this book.

And that's how a roller coaster of research became the book *Something Rotten: A Fresh Look at Roadkill.*

Inquiry is my life.

And you know what? I feel sorry for kids who don't get that.

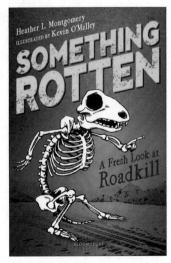

 Carla Killough McClafferty

Carla Killough McClafferty is an award-winning author of nonfiction books. She is a popular speaker at schools and teacher conferences both in person and via video conferencing. Her books have been recognized for excellence with starred reviews in *Booklist*, *Publishers Weekly*, *School Library Journal*, and more. She is an active member of iNK Think Tank, which produces *The Nonfiction Minute* podcast. Visit her website at carlamcclafferty.com.

Nonfiction Mentor Texts

Grades 6–8; LF; Bio/SS, Bio/STEM

McClafferty, Carla Killough. *Buried Lives: The Enslaved People of George Washington's Mount Vernon.* New York: Holiday House, 2018.

———. *In Defiance of Hitler: The Secret Mission of Varian Fry.* New York: Farrar, Straus and Giroux, 2008.

———. *Something Out of Nothing: Marie Curie and Radium.* New York: Farrar, Straus and Giroux, 2006.

Fragments of My Own Life

Tragedy made me a writer.

My fourteen-month-old son, Corey, died from a head injury after a minor fall off the backyard swing. Life as I knew it was over. I faced a crisis of faith that took time to work through. Although I'd never written before, I knew I was supposed to share my experiences. I wrote a deeply personal book for adults titled *Forgiving God: A Woman's Struggle to Understand When God Answers No.*

After that book, I continued writing. I believed I could write about the lives of other people and keep my own emotions unattached and a safe distance away. I was wrong. I soon discovered that I'd use the fire of my own emotions to choose topics and write about them in a way that only I could.

When I was doing the research for *Something Out of Nothing: Marie Curie and Radium*, my mother was dying of cancer. On nights I spent beside her hospital bed, I filled my sleepless hours reading research material. I searched for the best way to make a reader understand that inside the always stern-looking Curie beat the heart of a vulnerable woman who had faced a lot of adversity. While I grieved the loss of my own loved ones, I wrote about the day Marie's husband, Pierre Curie, died. Tears flowed down my cheeks as I wrote and rewrote that scene. Even today I tear up when I read the words I wrote.

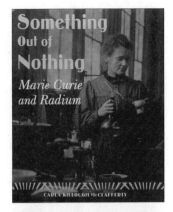

As I searched for the topic of my next book, a photograph I'd seen once lurked in the back of my mind. It was of Nazi soldiers surrounding an elderly Jewish man, laughing as they cut off his beard. I started researching the Holocaust, looking for a true story that hadn't been told. When I found Varian Fry, I knew that was the book I had to write.

Fry was an American journalist who volunteered to go to Marseilles, France, in 1940 to rescue Jewish refugees trapped there. As I researched *In Defiance of Hitler: The Secret Mission of Varian Fry*, I studied Hitler's rise to power and the war in Europe. While writing the text, I chose each word carefully so that my readers would be transported to the streets of Marseilles in 1940. I want readers to feel the fear and desperation of the refugees who were trapped there. I want them to understand how Varian Fry and his team felt as they made life-and-death choices about who they could help and who they couldn't.

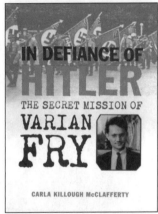

As a writer, I must feel the emotions first (oh yes, I feel them). Then, I hope, my readers will feel them, too.

I tackled another difficult topic in *Buried Lives: The Enslaved People of George Washington's Mount Vernon*. In it, I highlight the lives of six enslaved people who served the Washington family. During the five years I spent writing the book, I felt a host of emotions as I thought about the lives of each one. I hope my readers will see these six individuals as real, flesh-and-blood people with the same feelings we have today. I want them to step out of the fog of history to stand in the spotlight.

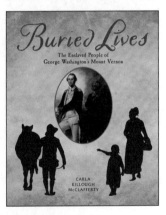

As every nonfiction book should be, my books are filled with the facts. But along with the facts, I do my best to deliver maximum emotional impact. I want readers to FEEL my books.

At the beginning of my career, I didn't know how deeply I would need to dig into my own emotional life to write about the lives of others. When I look back through my books, I recognize tiny fragments of myself scattered across the pages.

In the Classroom

As I mentioned in the introduction, many of the mentor essays in this book could have been placed in more than one chapter. If you go back and skim some of your favorite essays from Chapters 1 and 2, you'll see that the importance of making personal connections emerges again and again. And, of course, that idea comes through loud and clear in all seventeen essays in this chapter.

Who nonfiction writers are as people and their experiences in the world have a tremendous impact on how they evaluate, assimilate, analyze, and synthesize their research to make their own meaning. Each writer views the facts and ideas they collect through their own lens, and that's what allows them to present information in unique and interesting ways. It's the reason that *Death Eaters: Meet Nature's Scavengers* by Kelly Milner Halls is so different from *Rotten! Vultures, Beetles, Slime, and Nature's Other Decomposers* by Anita Sanchez and *Something Rotten: A Fresh Look at Roadkill* by Heather L. Montgomery even though all three books have some overlapping content.

Currently, most students don't take time to think before they write. They don't evaluate, assimilate, analyze, or synthesize the information they've gathered. And because this critical step isn't part of their prewriting process, they sometimes end up plagiarizing. But when students learn to add a piece of themselves to their drafts, they can move beyond writing dry, encyclopedic survey pieces that mimic their sources and begin crafting rich, distinctive prose. Here are some strategies to help students make their writing more personal.

Strategy 1: Sources They Can't Copy

When it's time to write nonfiction, most students turn to books and the internet for information, but professional writers know that these sources are just the tip of the iceberg. For us, gathering research is like a treasure hunt—a quest for tantalizing tidbits of knowledge. It's an active, self-driven process that requires a whole lot of innovative thinking. We want our books to feature fascinating facts and intriguing ideas that no one else has ever written about. To find that information, we think creatively about sources. We ask ourselves:

Who can I ask?

Where can I go?

How can I search in a new or unexpected way?

Unfortunately, most students don't bring this same creative spirit to their research, and that's why they often find it boring.

Research should be as varied and wide ranging as possible, and it should include sources that can't be copied, such as firsthand observations made in person or via webcams. Students can also watch documentary films, examine artifacts, and interview experts. While the idea of asking students to conduct interviews might seem daunting, it doesn't have to be if your school takes the time to develop a community of experts. Everyone is an expert in something. By surveying parents at the beginning of the year, the school can build a database that includes what parents and staff members are passionate about and whether they're willing to answer questions from a child doing a report. You can also identify community workers who are willing to assist students. It's a great way to help children understand how professional writers go about their work. And because students develop their own questions and record the answers, the information they collect will be imaginative and original. When students do this kind of research, there's no chance of plagiarism.

Strategy 2: Pause and Ponder

Teachers today have so much to accomplish, so much material to cover in just 180 days. Since every minute counts, it may seem like a waste of time to add another step to the student writing process. But it makes a difference. When students pause and ponder before they start writing, they're able to take ownership of the material and formulate a plan. This kind of preparation builds enthusiasm, and, in many cases, it makes drafting go more smoothly and reduces the amount of time students spend revising.

Teaching Tip

The best student writing happens when the teacher participates in the activity. When you write alongside your class, it shows that you value the process. You can ask questions as a colleague and help guide student thinking. And you can model techniques that may initially seem confusing or uncomfortable to students. Most importantly, you demonstrate that writers at all levels are always looking for ways to improve.

Begin by asking students to read through their notes and circle facts and ideas that seem interesting and important. Then encourage them to use one of the thought prompts discussed in Chapter 2 (see page 115), or simply have them make a list of the information they circled.

After sharing quotations from several of the mentor essays included in this chapter, try asking students to think about the information using their head (their brain) *and* their heart (their feelings). Then invite them to spend a few minutes freewriting and sketching. This gives young writers time and space to digest the information, view it through their own lens, and make their own meaning.

Finally, encourage students to create an infographic that includes what they really want other people to know about their topic and why that aspect of the

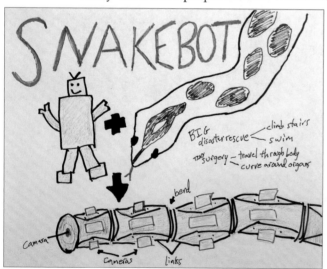

topic is important to them. The infographic could also show the order in which they plan to present the information, but it doesn't have to.

When students take the time to represent key parts of their research as infographics during the prewriting process, they'll find their own special way of conveying the information. Instead of being tempted to plagiarize, they'll create prose that's 100 percent their own.

Strategy 3: Adding a Piece of Themselves

This activity is recommended for students in grades 4–8 who have considerable writing experience and have practiced techniques like Pause and Ponder.

Preactivity

In many schools, students are used to following specific instructions. They've been taught to think that there's only one right way to do things and only one right answer to a question. But in this activity, students must think imaginatively and independently. Every child will have a different answer, and they're all correct.

If you think your students are ready for this kind of challenge, you can skip ahead to the Prep Step. But if your students could use some practice thinking in this way, try the following preactivity, which is modified from a technique I learned from author Helaine Becker.

Pass out white drawing paper and ask students to draw a circle. If they ask questions, such as "How big should it be?" or "In the center of the page?," tell them that it's their decision. In this activity, there is no wrong answer.

Next, ask students to draw a line inside the circle. If they ask questions, repeat that it's up to them. Encourage them to use their imagination.

Finally, ask the students to draw a picture that incorporates the circle. If they ask questions, repeat that it's up to them; they should use their imagination.

When the class seems ready, invite a few student volunteers to share their drawings. Then ask the following questions:

- How did it feel to make these kinds of decisions on your own?
- How is who you are as a person—your interests, your thoughts, your experiences—reflected in your drawing?
- How do you think the drawings would be different if I had given more instructions?

Following a brief class discussion, let your students know that they're going to do a writing activity similar to the drawing activity. They'll be using their imagination and making their own decisions. Everyone's writing will be different, but no one will be wrong.

Prep Step

When your class has a bit of free time, pass out photocopies of the Flesh Fly Activity Sheet on page 176 and ask students to circle the group of facts they find most interesting. Students will refer back to this reproducible sheet as they complete the activity.

Flesh Fly Activity Sheet

Name: _____

This page has five bits of information. Please read them carefully and circle the one you think is most surprising or interesting. Then underline the part that made you say, "Oh, wow."

Flesh flies have a four-stage life cycle.
They spend 1 to 2 days as **eggs**.
They are **larvae** (maggots) for 4 to 7 days.
They spend 17 to 30 days as **pupa**.
Then they are **adults** for just 1 or 2 days.

An adult flesh fly has big, red eyes. Each eye has 3,000 lenses.
The lenses help the fly see in every direction.
That's why it's hard to sneak up on a fly.

Adult flesh flies usually feed on flower nectar.
They drink juices from rotting fruit, too.
They also sip liquids from animal poop and dead, rotting animals.

A female flesh fly lays about twelve eggs at a time.
When they hatch, she places the maggots on a harlequin toad's skin.
Then the larvae burrow into the toad and feed on its body.
This kills the toad in just a few days.

Flesh flies are fantastic fliers. They can fly up, down, forward, or backward. They can spin and hover, too. They can even do somersaults in the air and land upside down.

What's the secret to the fly's success? It has something other insects don't—halteres. These special body parts help a fly keep its balance and fine-tune its flight path.

Nonfiction Writers Dig Deep: 50 Award-Winning Children's Book Authors Share the Secret of Engaging Writing edited by Melissa Stewart © 2020 Melissa Stewart.

Activity

Begin the activity by sharing the personal connection that helped me shape *Pipsqueaks, Slowpokes, and Stinkers: Celebrating Animal Underdogs* (see page 118). Let students know that I was a clumsy, unathletic child, and that, in some ways, the double-page spread about the western fence lizard is autobiographical.

What's the world's clumsiest critter? Probably the western fence lizard. As it skitters along tree branches, it sometimes loses its balance and falls to the forest floor. *Thud.*

Why does the little lizard run so fast that it stumbles over its feet? Because it needs speed to catch quick-crawling spiders and insects. Wouldn't you rather take a tumble once in a while than starve to death?

Assure students that writers don't always have to dig so deep or add that much of themselves to their writing, but that personal connections can help writers feel more invested, which leads to better writing. Then share quotations from several of the mentor essays in this book, along with excerpts from the children's books those authors discuss.

When students begin to get a sense of how authors they admire make their writing personal, ask your class to take out the Flesh Fly Activity Sheet they completed earlier, choose one of the four writing prompts included in Chapter 2 (see page 115), and respond to it in their writer's notebook.

After a few student volunteers have shared their responses, lead them through the notebook work and writing samples I did as I was writing the flesh fly section of *Ick: Delightfully Disgusting Animal Dinners, Dwellings, and Defenses* (see pages 119–21).

Now it's your students' turn. Encourage them to brainstorm creative ways they could share the flesh fly information they selected on the Flesh Fly Activity Sheet. Then ask them to think of personal connections to the information. Ask students: How can you put a piece of yourself into your writing?

Teaching Tip

You can take photos of my notebook pages and writing samples and display them on the classroom interactive whiteboard, or you can use a document camera to share the images.

The writing students produce during this activity is often full of misspellings and grammatical errors, but that's okay. The goal isn't to produce perfectly polished prose. Even the actual words students put onto paper aren't that important. What matters is the ideas, the creativity, the personal connections that emerge.

It's also not unusual for students to write a lot of not-so-great text before they get to the bits of gold. It's important to point out any strong personal connections you see so that students know when they're on the right track.

This is hard work for students, so it may take a bit of encouragement and a whole lot of praise for them to get the hang of it. But once they do, the results will blow you away.

For example, in one fifth-grade class, a boy focused on karma (as in, it's about time flies got their revenge against toads) because that idea was important to his family and upbringing.

A girl on the other side of the room wrote a fun piece titled "Not Your Average Flesh Fly," inspired by her family's favorite restaurant—Not Your Average Joe's.

And another girl compared the flies to her cat. She explained that flesh flies are smaller than a toad and her cat is smaller than she is, but in both cases, the smaller animal has adaptations that allow it to "defeat" the larger one.

What great thinking!

While doing this activity once can be eye-opening for students, it's really a technique they should practice again and again using a wide variety of mentor texts. Like all the strategies in this book, it should become a regular part of your class's prewriting process. When students consistently have the opportunity to choose their own topics, find a focus they're excited about, and put the information they gather through their own personal filter to make their own meaning, their writing will shine.

Bibliography of Children's Books

Albee, Sarah. *Bugged: How Insects Changed History*. New York: Bloomsbury/Walker, 2014.

———. *Poison: Deadly Deeds, Perilous Professions, and Murderous Medicines*. New York: Crown/Penguin Random House, 2017.

———. *Poop Happened! A History of the World from the Bottom Up*. New York: Bloomsbury/Walker, 2010.

———. *Why'd They Wear That: Fashion as the Mirror of History*. Washington, DC: National Geographic, 2015.

Barton, Chris. *What Do You Do with a Voice Like That? The Story of Extraordinary Congresswoman Barbara Jordan*. San Diego, CA: Beach Lane/Simon & Schuster, 2018.

Bowman, Donna Janell. *Abraham Lincoln's Dueling Words*. Atlanta, GA: Peachtree, 2018.

———. *Step Right Up: How Doc and Jim Key Taught the World about Kindness*. New York: Lee & Low, 2016.

Carson, Mary Kay. *The Bat Scientists*. Boston: Houghton Mifflin Harcourt, 2010.

———. *Emi and the Rhino Scientist*. Boston: Houghton Mifflin Harcourt, 2010.

———. *Park Scientists: Gila Monsters, Geysers, and Grizzly Bears in America's Own Backyard*. Boston: Houghton Mifflin Harcourt, 2014.

Castaldo, Nancy F. *Beastly Brains: Exploring How Animals Think, Talk, and Feel*. Boston: Houghton Mifflin Harcourt, 2017.

———. *Sniffer Dogs: How Dogs (and Their Noses) Save the World*. Boston: Houghton Mifflin Harcourt, 2014.

———. *The Story of Seeds: Our Food Is in Crisis. What Will You Do to Protect It?* Boston: Houghton Mifflin Harcourt, 2020.

Chin, Jason. *Grand Canyon*. New York: Roaring Brook, 2017.

———. *Redwoods*. New York: Roaring Brook/Square Fish, 2009.

Cline-Ransome, Lesa. *Before She Was Harriet*. New York: Holiday House, 2017.

———. *Just a Lucky So and So: The Story of Louis Armstrong*. New York: Holiday House, 2016.

———. *Major Taylor, Champion Cyclist*. New York: Simon & Schuster/Atheneum, 2004.

———. *My Story, My Dance: Robert Battle's Journey to Alvin Ailey*. New York: Simon & Schuster/Paula Wiseman, 2015.

———. *Satchel Paige*. New York: Simon & Schuster, 2000.

———. *Words Set Me Free: The Story of Young Frederick Douglass*. New York: Simon & Schuster/Paula Wiseman, 2012.

———. *Young Pelé: Soccer's First Star*. New York: Schwartz & Wade, 2007.

Fishman, Seth. *A Hundred Billion Trillion Stars*. New York: Greenwillow, 2017.

Fleming, Candace. *Amelia Lost: The Life and Disappearance of Amelia Earhart*. New York: Penguin Random House/Schwartz & Wade, 2011.

———. *The Family Romanov: Murder, Rebellion, and the Fall of Imperial Russia*. New York: Penguin Random House/Schwartz & Wade, 2014.

———. *Giant Squid*. New York: Roaring Book, 2016.

———. *The Great and Only Barnum: The Tremendous, Stupendous Life of Showman P. T. Barnum*. New York: Penguin Random House/Schwartz & Wade, 2009.

———. *Honeybee: The Busy Life of* Apis mellifera. New York: Holiday House/Neal Porter Books, 2020.

———. *The Lincolns: A Scrapbook Look at Abraham and Mary*. New York: Penguin Random House/Schwartz & Wade, 2008.

Halls, Kelly Milner. *Death Eaters: Meet Nature's Scavengers*. Minneapolis, MN: Millbrook, 2018.

———. *Tales of the Cryptids: Mysterious Creatures That May or May Not Exist*. Minneapolis, MN: Millbrook, 2006.

Heiligman, Deborah. *The Boy Who Loved Math: The Improbable Life of Paul Erdös*. New York: Roaring Brook, 2013.

———. *Charles and Emma: The Darwins' Leap of Faith*. New York: Square Fish, 2011.

———. *From Caterpillar to Butterfly*. New York: HarperCollins, 1996.

———. *Vincent and Theo: The van Gogh Brothers*. New York: Henry Holt, 2017.

Hood, Susan. *Ada's Violin: The Story of the Recycled Orchestra of Paraguay*. New York: Simon & Schuster, 2016.

———. *Shaking Things Up: 14 Young Women Who Changed the World*. New York: Harper-Collins, 2018.

———, and Pathana Sornhiran. *Titan and the Wild Boars: The True Cave Rescue of the Thai Soccer Team*. New York: HarperCollins, 2019.

Jarrow, Gail. *Bubonic Panic: When Plague Invaded America*. Honesdale, PA: Boyds Mills/Calkins Creek, 2016.

———. *Fatal Fever: Tracking Down Typhoid Mary*. Honesdale, PA: Boyds Mills/Calkins Creek, 2015.

———. *Red Madness: How a Medical Mystery Changed What We Eat*. Honesdale, PA: Boyds Mills/Calkins Creek, 2014.

———. *Spooked! How a Radio Broadcast and* The War of the Worlds *Sparked the 1938 Invasion of America*. Honesdale, PA: Boyds Mills/Calkins Creek, 2018.

Judge, Lita. *Bird Talk: What Birds Are Saying and Why*. New York: Roaring Brook, 2012.

———. *Born in the Wild: Baby Mammals and Their Parents*. New York: Roaring Brook, 2014.

———. *Homes in the Wild: Where Baby Animals and Their Parents Live*. New York: Roaring Brook, 2019.

———. *How Big Were Dinosaurs?* New York: Roaring Brook, 2013.

———. *Play in the Wild: How Baby Animals Like to Have Fun*. New York: Roaring Brook, 2020.

Keating, Jess. *Cute as an Axolotl: Discovering the World's Most Adorable Animals*. New York: Knopf, 2018.

———. *Gross as a Snot Otter: Discovering the World's Most Disgusting Animals*. New York: Knopf, 2019.

———. *Pink Is for Blobfish: Discovering the World's Perfectly Pink Animals*. New York: Knopf, 2016.

———. *Shark Lady: The True Story of How Eugenie Clark Became the Ocean's Most Fearless Scientist*. Naperville, IL: Sourcebooks Jabberwocky, 2017.

———. *What Makes a Monster? Discovering the World's Scariest Creatures*. New York: Knopf, 2017.

Kerley, Barbara. *A Cool Drink of Water*. Washington, DC: National Geographic, 2002.

———. *The Extraordinary Mark Twain (According to Susy)*. New York: Scholastic Press, 2010.

———. *A Home for Mr. Emerson*. New York: Scholastic Press, 2014.

———. *A Little Peace*. Washington, DC: National Geographic, 2007.

———. *Those Rebels, John and Tom*. New York: Scholastic Press, 2012.

———. *With a Friend by Your Side*. Washington, DC: National Geographic, 2015.

Lang, Heather. *Anybody's Game: Kathryn Johnston, the First Girl to Play Little League Baseball*. Chicago: Albert Whitman, 2018.

———. *Fearless Flyer: Ruth Law and Her Flying Machine*. Honesdale, PA: Boyds Mills/Calkins Creek, 2016.

———. *Swimming with Sharks: The Daring Discoveries of Eugenie Clark*. Chicago: Albert Whitman, 2016.

Levinson, Cynthia. *Hillary Rodham Clinton: Do All the Good You Can*. New York: HarperCollins/Balzer + Bray, 2016.

———. *Watch Out for Flying Kids! How Two Circuses, Two Countries, and Nine Kids Confront Conflict and Build Community*. Atlanta, GA: Peachtree, 2015.

———. *We've Got a Job: The 1963 Birmingham Children's March*. Atlanta, GA: Peachtree, 2012.

———. *The Youngest Marcher: The Story of Audrey Faye Hendricks, a Young Civil Rights Activist*. New York: Simon & Schuster/Atheneum, 2017.

Levinson, Cynthia, and Sanford Levinson. *Fault Lines in the Constitution: The Framers, Their Fights, and the Flaws That Affect Us Today*. Atlanta, GA: Peachtree, 2019.

Markel, Michelle. *Brave Girl: Clara and the Shirtwaist Makers' Strike of 1909*. New York: HarperCollins/Balzer + Bray, 2013.

———. *The Fantastic Jungles of Henri Rousseau*. Grand Rapids, MI: Eerdmans, 2012.

———. *Out of This World: The Surreal Art of Leonora Carrington*. New York: Harper Collins/Balzer + Bray, 2019.

McClafferty, Carla Killough. *Buried Lives: The Enslaved People of George Washington's Mount Vernon*. New York: Holiday House, 2018.

———. *In Defiance of Hitler: The Secret Mission of Varian Fry*. New York: Farrar, Straus and Giroux, 2008.

———. *Something Out of Nothing: Marie Curie and Radium*. Farrar, Straus and Giroux, 2006.

Montgomery, Heather L. *Something Rotten: A Fresh Look at Roadkill*. New York: Bloomsbury, 2018.

Newman, Patricia. *Eavesdropping on Elephants: How Listening Helps Conservation*. Minneapolis, MN: Millbrook, 2018.

———. *Sea Otter Heroes: The Predators That Saved an Ecosystem*. Minneapolis, MN: Millbrook, 2017.

———. *Zoo Scientists to the Rescue*. Minneapolis, MN: Millbrook, 2017.

Paquette, Ammi-Joan, and Laurie Ann Thompson. *Two Truths and a Lie: Forces of Nature*. New York: Walden Pond, 2019.

———. *Two Truths and a Lie: Histories & Mysteries*. New York: Walden Pond, 2019.

———. *Two Truths and a Lie: It's Alive!* New York: Walden Pond, 2018.

Partridge, Elizabeth. *Boots on the Ground: America's War in Vietnam*. New York: Viking, 2018.

———. "Nightly News." In Marc Aronson and Susan Campbell Bartoletti (Eds.), *1968: Today's Authors Explore a Year of Rebellion, Revolution, and Change*. Somerville, MA: Candlewick, 2018.

Paul, Baptiste, and Miranda Paul. *Adventures to School: Real-Life Journeys of Students from around the World*. New York: Little Bee, 2018.

———. *I Am Farmer: Growing an Environmental Movement in Cameroon*. Minneapolis, MN: Millbrook, 2019.

Paul, Miranda. *Nine Months: Before a Baby Is Born*. New York: Holiday House, 2019.

Robeson, Teresa. *Queen of Physics: How Wu Chien Shiung Helped Unlock the Secrets of the Atom*. New York: Sterling, 2019.

Rockliff, Mara. *Anything but Ordinary Addie: The True Story of Adelaide Herrmann, Queen of Magic*. Somerville, MA: Candlewick, 2016.

———. *Born to Swing: Lil Hardin Armstrong's Life in Jazz*. Honesdale, PA: Boyds Mills/Calkins Creek, 2018.

———. *Lights! Camera! Alice! The Thrilling True Adventures of the First Woman Filmmaker*. San Francisco: Chronicle, 2018.

Rosenstock, Barb. *Otis and Will Discover the Deep: The Record-Setting Dive of the Bathysphere*. New York: Little, Brown, 2018.

———. *Prairie Boy: Frank Lloyd Wright Turns the Heartland into a Home*. Honesdale PA: Boyds Mills/Calkins Creek, 2019.

———. *Thomas Jefferson Builds a Library*. Honesdale, PA: Boyds Mills/Calkins Creek, 2013.

———. *Through the Window: Views of Marc Chagall's Life and Art*. New York: Knopf, 2018.

Salas, Laura Purdie. *A Leaf Can Be . . .* Minneapolis, MN: Millbrook, 2012.

———. *Meet My Family! Animal Babies and Their Families*. Minneapolis, MN: Millbrook, 2018.

———. *A Rock Can Be . . .* Minneapolis, MN: Millbrook, 2015.

———. *Snowman – Cold = Puddle: Spring Equations*. Watertown, MA: Charlesbridge, 2019.

———. *Water Can Be . . .* Minneapolis, MN: Millbrook, 2014.

Sanchez, Anita. *Leaflets Three, Let It Be! The Story of Poison Ivy*. Honesdale, PA: Boyds Mills, 2015.

———. *Rotten! Vultures, Beetles, Slime, and Nature's Other Decomposers*. Boston: Houghton Mifflin Harcourt, 2019.

Sayre, April Pulley. *Bloom Boom!* San Diego: Beach Lane/Simon & Schuster, 2019.

———. *Did You Burp? How to Ask Questions (or Not!)*. Watertown, MA: Charlesbridge, 2019.

———. *Like a Lizard*. Honesdale, PA: Boyds Mills, 2019.

———. *Raindrops Roll*. San Diego: Beach Lane/Simon & Schuster, 2015.

———. *Thank You, Earth: A Love Letter to Our Planet*. New York: Greenwillow, 2018.

Sheinkin, Steve. *The Notorious Benedict Arnold: A True Story of Adventure, Heroism & Treachery*. New York: Flashpoint, 2010.

Shepard, Ray Anthony. *A Long Time Coming: The Ona to Obama Chronicles*. New York: Boyds Mills/Calkins Creek, 2022.

———. *Now or Never! 54th Massachusetts Infantry's War to End Slavery*. Honesdale, PA: Boyds Mills/Calkins Creek, 2017.

———. *Runaway: The Daring Escape of Ona Judge*. New York: Farrar, Straus and Giroux, 2021.

Silvey. Anita. *I'll Pass for Your Comrade: Women Soldiers in the Civil War*. New York: Clarion, 2008.

———. *Let Your Voice Be Heard: The Life and Times of Pete Seeger*. New York: Clarion, 2016.

———. *The Plant Hunters: True Stories of Their Daring Adventures to the Far Corners of the Earth*. New York: Farrar, Straus and Giroux, 2012.

———. *Undaunted: The Wild Life of Biruté Mary Galdikas and Her Fearless Quest to Save Orangutans*. Washington, DC: National Geographic, 2019.

———. *Unforgotten: The Wild Life of Dian Fossey and Her Relentless Quest to Save Mountain Gorillas*. Washington, DC: National Geographic, 2021.

———. *Untamed: The Wild Life of Jane Goodall*. Washington, DC: National Geographic, 2015.

Sorell, Traci. *We Are Grateful: Otsaliheliga*. Watertown, MA: Charlesbridge, 2018.

Stewart. Melissa. *Can an Aardvark Bark?* San Diego: Beach Lane/Simon & Schuster, 2017.

———. *Feathers: Not Just for Flying*. Watertown, MA: Charlesbridge, 2014.

———. *Ick! Delightfully Disgusting Animal Dinners, Dwellings, and Defenses*. Washington, DC: National Geographic, 2020.

———. *Pipsqueaks, Slowpokes, and Stinkers: Celebrating Animal Underdogs*. Atlanta, GA: Peachtree, 2018.

———. *A Place for Birds*. Atlanta, GA: Peachtree, 2015.

———. *Seashells: More Than a Home*. Watertown, MA: Charlesbridge, 2019.

———. *A Seed Is the Start*. Washington, DC: National Geographic, 2018.

Stone, Tanya Lee. *Almost Astronauts: 13 Women Who Dared to Dream*. Somerville, MA: Candlewick, 2009.

———. *Sandy's Circus: A Story about Alexander Calder*. New York: Viking, 2008.

Swanson, Jennifer. *Astronaut-Aquanaut: How Space Science and Sea Science Interact*. Washington, DC: National Geographic, 2018.

———. *Brain Games: The Mind-Blowing Science of Your Amazing Brain*. Washington, DC: National Geographic, 2015.

———. *Super Gear: Nanotechnology and Sports Team Up*. Watertown, MA: Charlesbridge, 2016.

Swinburne, Stephen R. *Run, Sea Turtle, Run: A Hatchling's Journey*. Minneapolis, MN: Millbrook, 2020.

———. *Sea Turtle Scientist*. Boston, MA: Houghton Mifflin Harcourt, 2014.

———. *Turtle Tide: The Ways of Sea Turtles*. Honesdale, PA: Boyds Mills, 2005.

Tate, Don. *It Jes' Happened: When Bill Traylor Started to Draw*. New York: Lee & Low, 2012.

———. *Poet: The Remarkable Story of George Moses Horton*. Atlanta, GA: Peachtree, 2015.

———. *Strong as Sandow: How Eugen Sandow Became the Strongest Man on Earth*. Watertown, MA: Charlesbridge, 2017.

Thompson, Laurie Ann. *Be a Changemaker: How to Start Something That Matters*. New York: Simon Pulse/Beyond Words, 2014.

———. *Emmanuel's Dream: The True Story of Emmanuel Ofosu Yeboah*. New York: Penguin Random House/Schwartz & Wade, 2015.

Turner, Pamela S. *Crow Smarts: Inside the Brain of the World's Brightest Bird*. Boston: Houghton Mifflin Harcourt, 2016.

———. *The Dolphins of Shark Bay*. Boston: Houghton Mifflin Harcourt, 2013.

Valdez, Patricia. *Joan Procter, Dragon Doctor: The Woman Who Loved Reptiles*. New York: Knopf, 2018.

Wallace, Sandra Neil. *Between the Lines: How Ernie Barnes Went from the Football Field to the Art Gallery*. New York: Paula Wiseman/Simon & Schuster, 2018.

———, and Rich Wallace. *First Generation: 36 Trailblazing Immigrants and Refugees Who Make America Great*. New York: Little, Brown, 2018.

Wallmark, Laurie. *Ada Byron Lovelace and the Thinking Machine*. Berkeley, CA: Creston, 2015.

———. *Grace Hopper: Queen of Computer Code*. New York: Sterling, 2017.

———. *Hedy Lamarr's Double Life: Hollywood Legend and Brilliant Inventor*. New York: Sterling, 2019.

Ward, Jennifer. *How to Find a Bird*. San Diego: Beach Lane/Simon & Schuster, 2020.

———. *I Love Birds! 52 Ways to Wonder, Wander, and Explore Birds with Kids*. Boulder, CO: Roost Books, 2019.

———. *Mama Built a Little Nest*. San Diego: Beach Lane/Simon & Schuster, 2014.

Weatherford, Carole Boston. *Becoming Billie Holiday*. Honesdale, PA: Wordsong, 2008.

———. *Birmingham, 1963*. Honesdale, PA: Wordsong, 2007.

———. *Freedom on the Menu: The Greensboro Sit-ins*. New York: Dial, 2004.

———. *The Legendary Miss Lena Horne*. New York: Atheneum, 2017.

———. *Moses: When Harriet Tubman Led Her People to Freedom*. New York: Hyperion, 2006.

———. *The Roots of Rap: 16 Bars on the 4 Pillars of Hip-Hop*. New York: Little Bee, 2019.

———. *Schomburg: The Man Who Built a Library*. Somerville, MA: Candlewick, 2017.

———. *Voice of Freedom: Fannie Lou Hamer, Spirit of the Civil Rights Movement*. Somerville, MA: Candlewick, 2015.

Wind, Lee. *No Way, They Were Gay? Hidden Lives and Secret Loves*. Minneapolis, MN: Zest Books/Lerner, 2021.

Yoo, Paula. *From a Whisper to a Rallying Cry: The Killing of Vincent Chin and the Trial that Galvanized the Asian American Movement.* New York: Norton Young Readers, 2021.

———. *Shining Star: The Anna May Wong Story.* New York: Lee & Low, 2009.

———. *Sixteen Years in Sixteen Seconds: The Sammy Lee Story.* New York: Lee & Low, 2005.

———. *Twenty-Two Cents: Muhammad Yunus and the Village Bank.* New York: Lee & Low, 2005.

Young, Karen Romano. *Antarctica: The World's Shrinking Continent.* London: What on Earth, 2021.

———. #AntarcticLog, antarcticlog.com.

———. *Try This! 50 Fun Experiments for the Mad Scientist in You.* Washington, DC: National Geographic, 2014.

———. *Try This! Extreme: 50 Fun & Safe Experiments for the Mad Scientist in You.* Washington, DC: National Geographic, 2017.

Professional References

Clark, S. K., Jones, C. D., & Reutzel, D. R. (2013). Using the text structures of information books to teach writing in the primary grades. *Early Childhood Education Journal,*
41(4), 265–71.

Dorfman, L. R., & Cappelli, R. (2009). *Nonfiction mentor texts: Teaching informational writ-*
ing through children's literature, K–8. Stenhouse.

Englert, C. S., & Hiebert, E. H., (1984). Children's developing awareness of text structures in expository material. *Journal of Educational Psychology, 76*(1), 65–74.

Hepler, S. (1998). Nonfiction books for children: New directions, new challenges. In R.
A. Bamford and J. V. Kristo (Eds.), *Making facts come alive: Choosing quality nonfiction*
literature K–8 (pp. 3–20). Christopher-Gordon.

Hinz, Carol. (n.d.). Nonfiction books and the creative process (Part 1). *The Lerner Blog.*
https://lernerbooks.blog/2018/01/nonfiction-books-creative-process-part-1.html

Keating, J. (2018, January 6). STORYSTORM 18: Jess Keating notices the amazing. *Writ-*
ing for kids (while raising them). https://taralazar.com/2018/01/06/storystorm-
2018-day-6-jess-keating/

Kerper, R. M. (1998). Choosing quality nonfiction literature: Features for accessing and
visualizing information. In R. A. Bamford and J. V. Kristo (Eds.), *Making facts come*
alive: Choosing quality nonfiction literature K–8 (pp. 55–74). Christopher-Gordon.

Kiefer, B. Z. (2010). *Charlotte Huck's children's literature.* McGraw-Hill Higher Education.

Moss, B. (2003). *Exploring the literature of fact: Children's nonfiction trade books in the elemen-*
tary classroom. Guilford Press.

Muzi, J. (2017). Road tested / Five ways to strengthen student questioning. *ASCD Edu-*
cation Update, 59(1). http://www.ascd.org/publications/newsletters/education-
update/jan17/vol59/num01/Five-Ways-to-Strengthen-Student-Questioning.aspx

Portalupi, J., & Fletcher, R. (2001). *Nonfiction craft lessons: Teaching informational writing*
K–8. Stenhouse.

Stewart, M., & Young, T. A. (2018). Defining and describing expository literature. In V.
Yenika-Agbaw, L. A. Hudock, & R. M. Lowery (Eds.), *Does nonfiction equate truth?*
Rethinking disciplinary boundaries through critical literacy (pp. 11–24). Rowman & Lit-
tlefield.

Williams, J. P., Nubla-Kung, A. M., Pollini, S., Stafford, K. B., Garcia, A., & Snyder, A. E. (2007). Teaching cause-effect text structure through social studies content to at-risk second graders. *Journal of Learning Disabilities, 40*(2), 111–20.

Index

....

Note: A *t* following a page number indicates a table; an *f* indicates a figure.

Editor

Melissa Stewart has written more than 180 science books for children, including the ALA Notable *Feathers: Not Just for Flying*, illustrated by Sarah S. Brannen; the SCBWI Golden Kite Honor title *Pipsqueaks, Slowpokes, and Stinkers: Celebrating Animal Underdogs*, illustrated by Stephanie Laberis; and *Can an Aardvark Bark?*, illustrated by Caldecott Honoree Steve Jenkins. She coauthored *5 Kinds of Nonfiction: Enriching Reading and Writing Instruction with Children's Books* (forthcoming) and grades K–2 and 3–5 editions of *Perfect Pairs: Using Fiction & Nonfiction Picture Books to Teach Life Sci-*  *ence*. Stewart maintains the award-winning blog *Celebrate Science* and serves on the Society of Children's Book Writers and Illustrators board of advisors. Her highly regarded website, https://www.melissa-stewart.com/, features a rich array of nonfiction writing resources.

This book was typeset in TheMix and Palatino by Barbara Frazier.

Typefaces used on the cover include Blair ITC, Knockout, Avenir Next, and DIN.

The book was printed on 60-lb. White Offset paper by Seaway Printing Company, Inc.